Speaking Geek

The ABC's of Technology

by Bob Cohen

www.bobology.com

Speaking Geek

The ABC's of Technology Terms

www.bobology.com

Why This Book? 1

The Basics 3

Computers, Networks, and the Internet 3

Companies and Standards 5

Computers and Devices...............9

What are Computers?...9

What are Devices? 11

What is a Bit and a Byte?...................................13

What is a Motherboard? 15

What is RAM? 18

What is USB?...21

What is a Pixel?...23

What is an Ebook? 24

Software Programs 29

What is a Software Program? 29

Software Basics...29

What Are Software Updates and Upgrades? ...33

What is a File Extension?...................................35

What's a JPEG, GIF, PNG, and PDF?..............38

What's a Virus, Worm, and Trojan Horse?.......40

Networks and Connections 43

What is an IP Address? 43

What are Mbps and Bandwidth? 50

What is an ISP?...55

Wireless Networking 58

What is WiFi?...58

What is a HotSpot? 62

What Does 4G LTE Mean?................................64

Mobile 67

What is a Smartphone? 67

What is Android? 69

What is a Touchscreen?....................................71

What is Bluetooth? 76

What is GPS? 78

What is a SIM Card? 79

World Wide Web 81

What is a URL?....................................81

What is a Search Engine? 83

What is HTML?..................................84

What is a Domain?............................86

What is a Cookie?..............................88

What are Bookmarks..........................90

What is a Username?..........................90

What is a Strong Password 95

What is Streaming? 96

What is Opt-In?..................................99

Social Media 103

What is a Social Network?................103

What is a Viral Video? 110

The Cloud 113

What is the Cloud?............................113

What's a Server and a What's a Client? 114

What is Syncing?..............................117

More Tech Terms for Free........121

Why This Book?

The language of technology is changing how we communicate. To follow the plot on television shows it's necessary to understand an increasingly technical vocabulary. The average dinner conversation includes technology terms and job skills require a working knowledge of the language of technology.

News reports cover technology product announcements as major events. As an instructor of adult education programs, I explain a wide range of technology to people of all ages and technical backgrounds. Students taking my classes often ask me to explain a technical term when it's introduced in the lesson.

Learn More with the Free Weekly Newsletter

It's because of this need that I write a weekly newsletter (to subscribe go to **www.bobology.com** and sign up for the email newsletter) where I explain a technical term of the week. It's impossible to cover all the technical terms used in the English language, but this book will help you understand many of the most important ones, explained in as non-technical a language as possible.

The email newsletter is completely free and you can always unsubscribe at any time by clicking on an unsubscribe link.

Even if you know something about technology, you still might learn a few things. If you're an expert, use this book to help explain technology to people who need help understanding it.

I don't believe that technology should be a mystery to people. Yes, you need a special education to create and build it, but to use technology and understand how it works, I've had success explaining things to non-technical people. So let's start with the basics.

The Basics

Computers, Networks, and the Internet

Computer Hardware and Software

Computers are electronic devices that can perform calculations using instructions from software.
The computer is the hardware, while software is the instructions which tell the computer what to do. If you were in your kitchen making a meal, you would be the computer and the recipe which you're following would be the software. The recipe tells you what ingredients and utensils you need to use to physically prepare the meal. Follow one recipe and you might have a sandwich, follow a different one and you'd end up with a salad. You're the same person, but you're following different instructions for each meal.

Networks

For computers to communicate with each other they need connect to each other. When computers connect to other computers it's called a network. Networks make it possible for us to visit websites using the Internet. These websites are on computers located somewhere on the Internet and a network allows the computer that has the website to communicate with our computer. The Internet is one of the best know networks, since almost everyone with a computer uses it.

Wireless and Mobile

A network that doesn't need physical cables is called a wireless network. Wireless networks make it possible to move around with computers, and that's called mobile computing. You might use a form of computer called a smartphone, which is designed from the ground up to use wireless networks. Wireless networks eliminate the need to use a cable to connect a computer to a network. But wired, or wireless, it's still a network.

World Wide Web

While you and I use personal computers and other personal electronic devices, there are companies, governments, and educational organizations that use large computers and networks. When these computers and networks are connected to a public network called the Internet, they become part of the World Wide Web. The World Wide Web consists of every computer and network connection to the Internet. Since it's public, it's possible to send messages across the Internet from one computer to another. In contrast, a private network would only connect specific computers to each other and a private network would require the approval of the organization that owned the network in order to connect to it.

Social Media

With the World Wide Web making connections between computers easier, people can connect with each other using websites specially designed for this purpose. Since human beings are social by nature, Social Media has a become a popular use of the World Wide Web.

The Cloud

The cloud is a way of referring to computers that you can't see, but that you can connect to from your computer. They are somewhere up in the "sky," in the cloud. In fact they are in computer rooms somewhere on the ground, but you don't really know, or care where they are. As long as you can connect to them, it's possible for your computer to ask them to do things for you. All of these "things" have been lumped together in the term "the cloud." So as a result it's a bit confusing.

In reality, if you get directions from a website, use an online shopping cart to make a purchase, or use a backup service over the Internet, you're already using the cloud.

Companies and Standards

Companies make products and offer services, and their goal is to make a profit for their investors. Governments and industry organizations create standards. These don't always go well together.

Companies

Companies are in the business of trying to attract and retain customers and make as much profit as possible. Without profit, they can't continue to survive and grow. In our society, companies can create products, offer services, and attract customers. Build a better mousetrap and people will buy it. The more unique the product, the greater the opportunity to make a profit, since no other company has anything similar to offer to customers. This is capitalism and it's baked into our economic system.

When one company offers a smashing success, other companies see an opportunity to make money if they can come up with a better idea. As a result, competition between companies is created. Competition offers consumers choices, and it forces companies to continually innovate and offer new and better products and services to customers.

Proprietary Standards

One way companies try to hold on to customers is by offering products and services that create a lasting relationship, rather than a one-time purchase. If a customer invests in learning and using one company's products or services, the customer has made an investment that may cause them to think hard before switching to a competitor. In addition, there may be an investment of money in resources to use the product that would be lost if the customer switched to another brand of product or service.

An example of this is a razor blade. Buy one and you're usually committed to using replacement razors from the manufacturer of the blade handle. The money you'll spend on razor blades during the time you own that brand is many times more than the cost of the original blade. And if you buy and stock up on replacement blades, you're unlikely to switch until you use up any supply you have on hand. Another product that is like this is a computer printer. The profit is in the replacement ink and toner for the manufacturer. So what's this have to do with anything?

When a company is the only source of a product or service, they stand to make all the profit. When a company's product becomes so widely used it can become a standard by which all other products are measured. However, since no other company can offer it, the product or service is called "proprietary." There is nothing inherently wrong with a proprietary standard, but it means one company has all the control. This kind of standard is often called a "defacto" standard as well, since one company has control of the product that sets the industry standard.

Industry Standards

In contrast, when an group creates an product specification and allows many companies to manufacture products or offer services this is considered an industry standard. Sometimes companies co-operate and get together to set standards when they see that they would benefit from having an industry standard. Rather than compete and have products that might not work together from different manufacturers, they decide that it's better for profits to allow many companies to share the technology.

The companies that participate in making the standard representatives with the technical expertise to create the specifications. Then they offer other companies the ability to make products or services by paying a license fee to the industry group to use the specifications. Industry standards help us use networks to connect computers made by different manufacturers. Imagine if every computer make had their own type of cables for connecting a keyboard and mouse to a computer.

Your Role as Chief Information Officer

The job title of people who keep information technology working at large organizations is often the "Chief Information Officers," or CIO. If information technology is responsible for a missed payroll, having to stop the manufacturing line, or shut down a service, the Chief Information Officer often is blamed. In our homes and small businesses, we are our own Chief Information Officers since we write the check that pays the bills.

Just like the Chief Information Officer of a large organization, we depend on the companies who make our technology products and services. Something breaks, and we have to pay the bill and spend the time trying to figure out how to fix it. I suspect that some of you have spent some time trying to make technology work and it can be very frustrating. So what does this mean to you?

There's a valuable lesson about personal technology that can be learned from people who spend large amounts of money on technology. They try to minimize risk by using proven products and by keeping their technology as simple as possible. When there is a defacto standard or an industry standard, they often use that product or service, since it's got a large customer base. A large customer base means better support. CIO's also check out the support and resources of the company before they make any purchase.

Connecting products together from one company and making them work can sometimes be frustrating, but when you start connecting products and services from different companies together, you have a new job. The professionals in technology who make different company's products work together are called Integrators. And when you use products or services from different companies, you have become an Integrator. That means that if there is a problem where two different company's products don't work with each other, it's your job to fix it, or find someone who can.

Simplifying your technology is one way to make your life easier, and using products and services from companies who offer better support can make the difference between hours of frustration and going about your day. Chief Information Officers invest a lot of time learning about technology and the companies involved in them, and if you're reading this book, you're on the path to making better choices and opening up new possibilities.

Computers and Devices

What are Computers?

When you think of a computer you might think of a box with cables coming out of it, with a display monitor screen, a keyboard, and a mouse. These devices are commonly referred to as personal computers or PC's.

What's Inside?

All personal computers include electronic components connected via cables and electronic connections using boards that hold the components, called Printed Circuit Boards, or when used with a computer, a Motherboard (explained later). The major parts of a computer include a processor chip, called a Central Processing Unit, that performs the calculations. It's a complicated electronic circuit that is on a single silicon chip. The CPU is the "brain" of the personal computer and runs everything.

In order to perform calculations, a computer needs a place to store it's work, which is memory. Different types of storage technologies are used to make the most of price versus speed. Faster speed usually cost more when you're dealing with technology. The fastest memory is called RAM (explained later), while the hard disk drive is the slower memory, but it much less expensive.

So inside we have a a board, a CPU, memory, and a hard disk drive. The connections to the outside world include various connectors where cables and connectors can be plugged in to let devices communicate with the computer.

Just as a note, desktops usually have additional slots for connecting add-on circuits. This is used to extend the capability or enhance the performance. Common add-on circuit cards include graphics cards for faster game performance, cards with special connectors, and sound cards for more sophisticated audio recording and playback.

A laptop is a form of personal computer that is portable and includes a built-in screen, keyboard, and mouse. It's essentially the same type of device as a personal computer but is more portable.

What's Outside?

The connectors include ways to connect an external display device, usually the monitor. Monitors are made in various sizes and display ratios. A traditional screen has a ratio of 4 units wide to 3 units high, like an older model TV. Since many users now use computers to play movies and video, many monitors have a widescreen ration, which is 16 units wide by 9 units high. This is the standard ration for High-Definition TV. It's even possible with the right connectors on a TV and a computer to connect the computer to a TV display and use it for the monitor.

In addition to the monitor, a personal computer has a keyboard and a mouse. These are called Human Interface Devices and are necessary for a person to use a personal computer. The computer doesn't really need them, but people do.

Peripherals

Additional connectors are usually available which allow connections to external devices, called peripherals. They are called peripherals because they aren't inside the personal computer case, they are peripheral to it. Common peripherals include printers and speakers, but there are thousands of devices made that will connect to a personal computer.

The ability to connect peripherals to a personal computer can change an average everyday computer into a point-of-sale cash register with a credit card swiper and a cash drawer. The ability to connect peripherals to a personal computer has been one of the reasons they have become so widely used.

OK, so this is a personal computer, and you probably own one or have at least used one. But lately you might be hearing the term "devices." In fact, Microsoft announced that it was reorganizing its whole organization recently and one part of the organization includes "devices."

What are Devices?

A device is a computer that simply isn't a personal computer. It includes a CPU, memory, and a way for a person to use the device. A device can do many, if not all, of the things a personal computer can do because it is a computer by any other name. It's called a device because it just doesn't have the traditional case, monitor, keyboard, and mouse we often associate with a personal computer. In a way, devices are to computers like breeds are to dogs.

Your already probably familiar with what a dog it, so let me draw a little comparison between computers and dogs. Dogs are four legged mammals with fur that are all descendants of a type of wolf. Humans, through breeding, have created all kinds of breeds of dogs in an amazing assortment of sizes, shapes, colors, and temperaments. But chances are you can recognize a dog when you see one, regardless of what breed it is. Devices are like the different breeds of dogs, only they are different breeds of computers, and we haven't stopped making up new ones.

Common Devices

The most common devices are tablets and smartphones, but devices can also come in other forms. Let's take on tablets, smartphones and look at some other "devices." Tablets Apple is credited with making the tablet popular with its iPad product, and now there are other manufacturers of tablet devices since they have become a popular form of computer. Tablets are a computer, with a CPU, storage, and a screen. The screen uses a technology called a "touchscreen" (explained later in the mobile section) and a person uses the tablet by touching the screen. The touch causes the device to respond.

What's happened is that your fingers have become the mouse and your taps are the equivalent of mouse clicks. The keyboard is part of the display, and when it appears your fingers can make contact with the display to enter text. So tablets have all the major parts of a personal computer, which include a CPU, memory, storage, along with a display, keyboard, and "mouse" which is your finger contact. If this sounds a lot like a personal computer, you've got the right idea since a tablet is at it's most basic definition another physical form of a computer.

Smartphones

Smartphones (explained in more detail later in the mobile section) are phones that do more than just make phone calls. The popular definition of a smartphone is a device with a CPU, storage, a touchscreen, and includes it's own phone number for making and receiving phone calls. It's actually just another type of computer. These are smaller than a tablet (so you can hold it up to your ear to make a phone call), and include a built-in phone. Think of a smartphone as a portable computer with a phone function built-in and you've got the right idea. So maybe you know about tablets and smartphones and are willing to accept that they are "devices" that are really just a different size and shape. But there are more devices out there.

Other Devices

There are other types of devices besides smartphones and tablets which are computers. They don't fit the traditional definition of a personal computer, and they aren't a tablet, or a smartphone, but they have the basics of a computer. Often these are computers dedicated to a specific function or a type of activity. Game consoles, which are pretty common, are one type of device you might know about, and these are computers designed specifically to play games. The Sony Playstation, Microsoft XBox, and the Nintendo Wii are common Game Consoles. They have a CPU, memory, use game controllers instead of a keyboard/ mouse, and typically use a television as a display.

As the power of computing hardware improves, devices sometimes cross over into other functions. And this is blurring the lines of computing. Devices can include forms of computers that might already exist such as a game console, but you might be hearing about "wearable" computers. Google already has produced a set of glasses with a computer built-in, and several hardware manufacturers have announced plans for a "watch" device.

I visited a dog show recently and was amazed at the number of breeds of dogs. All of these sizes, shapes, colors, and temperaments are dogs, and you can probably recognize a dog when you see one. Computers are a lot like dog breeds. Remember, as long as it has a CPU, memory, and it does calculations of some sort, it's a computer by any other name.

What is a Bit and a Byte?

The terms bit and byte refer to the value of information used in a computer. Digital computers use data in which each piece of information has a value of one or zero. You can think of these values as the position of a switch.

The number one represents the switch when it is on; the zero represents the switch when it is off. In fact, computers use miniature circuits, which are actually tiny switches. Computers can turn many switches on and off at a single time, which is why it can count faster than your fingers by using light switches.

Computers Know Two Numbers

Computers (and when I say computers I mean any type of computing device) use this system of counting with only two numbers, called binary, because a number can only be a zero or a one. It just doesn't know any other numbers. You're most familiar with using a decimal system, where a single digit can be 0 through 9. The 10 possible ways to write a single piece of information, 0, 1,2,3,4, 5, 6, 7, 8,and 9 represent the 10 digits.

Combine more than one decimal place, and you've got a lot of possible number combinations. To a computer's way of thinking a binary number is a bit, and it calculates using combinations of bits.

Since a computer can change a bit from a zero to one and back again so fast, it's able to perform calculations without even knowing that there's a number larger than 1.

Bits and Bytes

Since one digit is a bit of information, like a zero or one, more than one digit of information creates what's called a byte of information. In our familiar decimal counting system using 0 through 9, when you count to ten you need to add a second digit. SInce bits can only be zeros or ones (off and on to a computer), to count beyond 1, another digit is necessary. Then you create a combination of two digits which can be either zeros or ones. For example, 01 or 10. Since we're talking bits, 10 is not 10, but the rules of counting with zero and one, called the binary number system, tell us that 10, in decimal numbers, is the number

2. Add more places and it's possible to create larger numbers to be used in calculations.

This is what a byte does for a computer, it combines more than one place, or bit, to create a combination of zeros and ones that represent a larger number. Combining eight bits together creates a byte consisting of eight bits. Bytes allow computers to calculate faster since the byte is more complex information that just a single bit.

Software is a Translator

Software is the secret sauce that takes bits and bytes and translates them so that more information can be represented by zeros and ones. When software is used, it can translate a document on a computer screen into complex combinations of zeros and ones that the computer can understand and manipulate. Software combines bits and bytes to make something better. Just like you have ingredients in your kitchen like milk, bread, jelly, and peanut butter, when they are combined you make a sandwich. Software combines the zeros and ones together to create documents, display videos, send email, and more, but it's all done in zeros and ones.

It's a Digital World

Counting in binary is easy for a computer because a computer can do basic detections of the numbers 0 and 1 extremely fast. For humans, this is quite tedious. It was necessary to come up with other ways of hand writing information that utilized both letters and numbers to represent the data put into a computer. The fact is that still, today, one BIT of data represents one single piece, or a bit, of information.

What is a Motherboard?

A motherboard is a circuit board with electronic components that allow it to connect all the hardware of a computer together. It is a critical piece of hardware upon which every computer is built.

It's called a motherboard because its the main chassis in any computer. All the electronic components and hardware that make up the computer connect in some way to the motherboard. Any other circuit boards necessary to build a complete computer are referred to as "daughter" boards. Most personal computers that are built today don't have daughter boards and only use a motherboard, so you don't see the term "daughterboard" used very often.

What a Motherboard Does

Think of a computer as if it were a human body. The motherboard would be the skeleton. It doesn't do much on its own, but without it the body cannot function. Other pieces of hardware perform specific functions -- the heart pumps blood, the lungs breathe and the brain regulates everything -- while the skeleton supports them all. This is how a motherboard functions in a computer. It supports and connects the rest of the hardware. Unlike the body, of course, the heart, lungs or brain of a computer could be swapped out with more powerful versions that still connect perfectly to the skeleton.

Every computer and computer-like device has a motherboard. A television is controlled by a motherboard that has all of its parts permanently connected. You can't open up your television and upgrade its ability to display images. Smartphones are the same, with every necessary piece fixed in place. Laptop computers have most of the parts built-in to the motherboard in order to save space. No one would buy a laptop the size of a desktop PC.

Built-in Components and Upgrades

A basic motherboard can consist of only the electronic wiring necessary to connect all the components of a computer together. Components, like a processor and

RAM are then added to the motherboard to build the computer. To make computers less expensive, or to make them smaller, such as a mobile smartphone, motherboards can include some of the additional components as built-in pieces.

Personal computer motherboards often include built-in sound and graphics components, eliminating the need to add them as a separate pieces. This lowers the cost and size of the computer. If a motherboard is custom-built for a manufacturer, such as a tablet or smartphone, capabilities such as GPS or WiFI might be added to the motherboard. It just depends on who makes the motherboard. Most desktop PC's use motherboard that do not include the processor, which is added separately by the manufacturer. These motherboards can also be purchased as separate parts if you want to build your own computer.

Desktop PCs have the advantage of upgrades. The motherboard in a desktop has special slots where accessory cards can be inserted. Using accessory cards that can be installed, additional capabilities can be added to the computer for special uses. Some common examples are audio cards, graphics cards, and cards for special connectors. Using accessory cards, a desktop offers the most expandable motherboard. Laptops, smartphones, and tablets don't have the space for any additional circuit cards to be plugged in, so any additional accessories have to connect to external connectors.

Connections

Connectors are a part of every motherboard. This is how you might connect a printer to a USB connector, an ethernet cable to an ethernet connector, a keyboard, monitor, mouse, and other devices. The motherboard holds the connectors and provides the electrical connection to the rest of the computer. You just usually see the external connector.

Without a motherboard, there is no computer. A PC, smartphone, tablet, or any computing device would be nothing more than a fancy metal and plastic box filled with useless parts. The motherboard is what connects all the pieces together.

What is RAM?

RAM, or "random access memory," is the temporary storage space used by a computer while it's performing tasks. It is smaller both physically and in capacity than more permanent forms of data storage, such as hard or disk drives, but it can store and retrieve data much more quickly.

Why RAM is Used in Computers

Think of RAM as open shelf space that can hold data close at hand for fast, immediate access while you are doing work on your computer. Your computer has large amounts of information, or data, stored permanently in files on its hard drive. When you open up an application (software) ~ for example, the word processor or email ~ your CPU (central processing unit) is going to need room to store the data while doing its work with the application. But space on the CPU is limited. This is where RAM comes in. RAM is designed to allow its data to be accessed quickly, at very high speeds more closely matching the processing speed of the CPU. However, this access speed is gained at the cost of stability and permanence, because data on RAM is available only as long as the computer is turned on; lose the power and the data is erased.

What More RAM Does for You

The more memory a computer has, the more tasks it can perform simultaneously. Like anything else, RAM has both advantages and disadvantages when it comes to storing information. To evaluate these in greater detail, it can help to compare RAM memory to other types of memory storage available for computers.

When you determine that your computer needs more storage room, also known as memory, for additional data and software, you will have to decide which kind of storage will work the best for your needs.

How are RAM and Disk Drives Different?

Disk drives are one storage source for software and data. These have the advantage of storing large amounts of data relatively inexpensively. But they move data at slower speeds than RAM or CPU memory.

RAM is the storage choice when speed and efficiency are the paramount considerations. RAM is one of the easiest parts of a computer to upgrade, and gives the most obvious and immediate benefits. It is available as cards of memory modules that insert directly into computer circuit boards and comes in various speeds, sizes, and designs to better match specific computer types. However, RAM requires power to store data, which means that, unlike long-term storage systems like hard-disk drives that retain data, you lose RAM data whenever you turn off your computer. It may be fast, but it's temporary.

What is a Flash Drive?

When you use a computer, there are certain devices you will probably become familiar with. One of these is a flash drive. A flash drive is a small device that contains a USB connection on one end so that it can be attached to a desktop or laptop computer. It is small enough to stick in your pocket or purse so that you can tote it around. Some flash drives even have rings on the end so that you can attach them to your key ring.

In a nutshell, a flash drive is used to store content from your computer that you want to have in a separate drive. It is similar to an external hard drive, except that it is much smaller and has considerably less storage space. A flash drive can be available in storage amounts of 4GB, 8GB, 16GB, 32GB and, most recently, 64GB. You can buy them at any electronics store.

Who Uses a Flash Drive?

A flash drive is most often used by someone who needs to keep certain documents with him no matter where he goes. For instance, if you are a student who needs to present a homework assignment on a computer at school, or if you work in an office and need to take work home with you, a flash drive can be your best friend. Many people use flash drives as a backup for saving documents, images and other data in a place separate from or in addition to their computer's internal drive or standard external hard drive. A flash drive also allows you to share whatever you have saved on it with another person on her or his computer.

How do You Use a Flash Drive?

To use a flash drive on a PC, you merely need to plug it into any USB port on the computer. When the computer recognizes it, a new small window will appear with the words "Removable Disk" at the top. The "Open Folder to View Files" option will appear at the very bottom of the page. To view your files, click on that line. You can also add, remove or modify content that is saved to your flash drive. If you wish to remove your flash drive, go to your computer's Start menu, click on "Computer" and a new window will appear. Right-click on the drive containing your flash drive and select "Eject."

For use on a Mac, plug the flash drive into a USB port, then open up Finder. Your drive appears in a list under the heading called "Devices." Simply click on the flash drive (could appear under any of a number of names ~ if it isn't clear, then check around a bit) and it will take you to the files on the drive. To remove the flash drive from a Mac, click on the "Eject" icon next to the flash drive in Finder.

Be aware that flash drives should never be simply yanked out of your computer when the power is on. Always follow the above directions.

What is USB?

USB, which stands for universal serial bus, is a component that allows devices to be connected to computers. A desktop or laptop computer, mp3 player and most smartphones feature the female port of a USB. A male USB connector is needed to connect these devices for usage or charging.

What Can You Do with USB?

A USB port on a computer allows you to connect things such as an external hard drive, mouse, or printer to your desktop or laptop. Devices which connect to computers are often referred to as peripherals, because they work with the computer. But USB can be used to connect all types of devices to computers, including cameras, and smartphones, all that's needed is a USB connector on both devices.

USB: Speed and Now More Power!

All USB devices use a specific standard that allows them to function at a particular speed. The current standard for USB is 3.0, which offers transmission speeds of up to 5 Gbps. The previous standard, USB 2.0, provided speeds of only 480 Mbps. In addition to the USB connection speed, the standard applies to the size and shape of the USB connectors. USB can also supply power to a device connected to a computer or power adapter.

Many smartphones and tablets use a charging cable with a USB connector that plugs into a charging adapter for power, and your computer supplies a little power to every device connected to it with USB. In fact, USB battery packs are now available that can even recharge mobile devices and range from small to very large capacity, like the one shown on the right.

In the case of smartphones, the USB technology is the same but the connector may be smaller: many such phones feature a mini USB port and come with cable connectors with mini USB male parts. This is most likely to accommodate the smaller size of a smartphone. It allows you to sync your phone on your computer and, through USB, you can easily add files from your hard drive, such as music and images, to your smartphone.

USB Industry Forum

Devices which use the USB description must meet an industry standard specification that's managed by the USB Implementers Forum, a non-profit corporation founded by a group of companies. The USB Implementers Forum Board of Directors includes representatives from Hewlett-Packard, Microsoft, Intel, and other global technology companies. The purpose of this organization is to support the advancement and adoption of USB technology through education, device testing, and marketing. The benefit to you, the consumer, is an extensive choice of devices which all work together with one common connector. While it's not necessary for a product to be certified as "USB," the USB Implementers Forum does have a formal product certification program. The new "certified" logo, shown below, can only be used by those products which have passed certification testing.

USB Makes Connections Easier

Before USB became a widely adopted industry standard, connecting devices to computers wasn't always easy. I remember a time when I needed a different cable, adapter, and connector for each peripheral I had connected to my computer. Some of you may remember terms like "parallel" cable, DIP switches, and IRQ's. If so, you can see how far we've come in making technology easier with USB, since to add a peripheral now is so easy almost anyone can do it.

What is a Pixel?

The Pixel Dot

Pixels are tiny dots. No, we're not talking the candy kind. Pixels are those tiny dots that create what you see on computer displays (LCDs or flat screens) and tube monitors (CRT or desk top computers and digital TVs). Pixel means PICture ELement.

You can't see pixels because they're very small, which is good because you want to see the whole image and not those dots that make up the image (or pixilated images). Pixilated images are possible to see with your computer monitor screen set to a low resolution, such as 620x460, which means the product of width times height, for a total of 285,200 pixels, which may seem like a lot, but computer screens need more resolution to be clear and sharp.

Image Resolution

In a general sense, the more pixels used to represent an image equals a sharper image. Image resolution is measured by PPI, or pixels per inch. Resolution is also expressed in pairs of numbers such as 640 x 480 (width x length). A MacBook Pro 15-inch monitor, for example, has the PPI of 110 PPI and a 1440x900 resolution.

A basic digital camera has a resolution capacity of between 2 million pixels (MP) to 5 MP and the more pixels the better. A 4MP camera makes really sharp prints that are 4"x6" and pretty nice larger prints at 5"x7".

Pixel colors

Every single tiny pixel contains three color channels of red, green and blue. Each color in this scheme is represented by an 8-bit number, or a byte, with the color of each pixel defined by three color bytes. These three colors combine in over 16 million color combinations to form the many different hues and shades you see on your screen and camera.

For example, if an image contain the color depth of 8-bits, it will seem grainy or spotted. A 32-bit color image looks much more smooth and realistic.

Pixels Are Everywhere

It helps to know how pixels work because everything is digital these days, from your TV to your computer screen to your camera – even to the images you see displayed on your cell phone. You don't have to be a technological wizard to understand the basics so that you can get the best resolution for what you need and like.

What is an Ebook?

An ebook is just the digital form of a regular book. Instead of having an inch-thick novel in your hands, you have a file sitting in your computer, tablet, smartphone, or ebook reader.

You can read ebooks on your desktop or laptop, but if you want them to feel like the real thing, you can read them using your tablet instead. Tablets with a screen size of 7-inches are about the same size as a trade paperback, so you can at least pretend that you have a printed book in your hands.

Advantages of Ebooks

The great thing about ebooks is that you can have thousands of them in your ebook reader or tablet. You can switch between ebooks anytime you like. This surely beats standing up from your bed and reaching for a new book from the shelf. Also, think of the convenience when you travel! You don't have to lug around books in your hand-carry anymore.

If some printed books seem to have really tiny text that makes them hard to read, you can say goodbye to that problem. Another great thing about ebooks is that you can change the font size to suit your vision. You don't have to squint anymore to make out the words. Conversely, you can make the font smaller if you want to take in as much as you can in a single page.

When you want to buy ebooks, you don't have to go to the bookstore and look for the titles you like. Just log on to online stores and buy as many ebooks as you want from the comfort of your own home. And guess what? Ebooks are less expensive than printed books because they don't use paper to be mass-produced. Thus, you can sustain your bookworm lifestyle without hurting your budget.

Amazon started pushing ebooks when they started shipping their ebook reader, the Kindle. With a low cost, and with a screen   that uses e-ink, it made ebooks popular. Amazon just happened to be a very large online bookstore, and along with the Kindle device, Amazon has made sure that customers can access an extremely large collection of ebooks online. Amazon makes a free Kindle app available for Android and Apple devices, in addition to their own readers. Their approach to buying ebooks is "purchase once, read everywhere." So if you have an Apple or Android smartphone or tablet, you can read your Amazon books using the Kindle app.

Ebook Readers and Apps

In addition to Kindle devices, iPads, iPhones, Android tablets, and personal computers, there are a few other ways to purchase and read ebooks. Barnes & Noble offers ebooks through their Nook reader device, and the free Nook app is available for Apple and Android devices. Apple offers books through their iBooks app, and Google has books available from their Google Play store. Google even makes a reader app called Google Reader that works on Apple devices.

Public libraries offer ebook borrowing and have apps that usually work with Kindle, Apple, and Android mobile devices. Your local library can tell you what app they use and how to borrow ebooks from their collection.

Ebook Stores

Something to be aware of when buying an ebook from one store is that it you will likely need the app or device from that store to read your book. In order to keep you as a customer, some of the ebook stores don't let you read your ebook in another app or device. For example, any ebook you purchase on Amazon requires a Kindle reader or Kindle app, and your Amazon ebook can't be accessed by the iBook of Nook app.

Since Amazon, Google, and Nook are all available apps for Apple and Android devices, you just need to install the app on your tablet or device to read the book. A nook reader, however, won't be able to access your Amazon books. As a result, the iPad is the most versatile device since the iBook app is only available on Apple devices, and as a result, Apple devices have the widest selection of ebook reader apps.

However, since Amazon is such a large ebook store, Amazon still has the edge over all the other ebook stores in selection and availability of ebooks. As a result, many people have both a Kindle reader and a tablet. The Kindle is less expensive than a tablet and with the latest technology from Amazon, called Paperwhite, almost looks likes a printed page.

Earlier Kindles didn't have any built-in lighting, but newer models do, and make an excellent dedicated ebook reader which I still consider the best ebook reader on the market.

Printed Books Are Still OK

The printed book is still an excellent way to read. It's lightweight, portable, and many people still prefer the fresh smell of the pages of a new book. But you've got to admit that ebooks have their own uses and charm.

Software Programs

What is a Software Program?

A software program is the set of alphanumeric instructions that are given to computers and devices to perform calculations. Without software, our hardware wouldn't be able to do anything useful for us. Software is like a recipe for cooking. The recipe is a set of instructions for the cook, and includes steps for the cook to follow. Software is the recipe that computers need to work.

Software Basics

Software is written in alphanumeric characters with a format that uses specific characters to create instructions for the computer. When these instructions are complete enough for the computer to do something, the software becomes a program. Software Programs do work and perform calculations. Often software is also called "code" because the way the characters are used doesn't result in something that is written in English or any other common written or spoken language.

Code is the language of computers. Programmers are people who know how to read and write software programs written in computer languages. The English language is a code. If you put noun in front a verb, you can communicate a thought or idea to someone else who understands English. Combine letters in the right pattern and you create words, and words can describe things and actions.

Say "I ran" to another person who understands you, and they have an idea of what these characters mean. But say "X lggg" and you might not be able to communicate a thought or idea, unless someone knew your "code" and how you used the characters. Software, like spoken and written language, can be used to communicate. When software includes instructions that perform a task, the software becomes a program.

Applications

An application is a software program that includes instructions for doing tasks that a person might find useful. For example, a word processor application is a program. It includes many tasks and functions that cause the computer to respond when we use the program. People who understand how to write instructions using software are called programmers. We depend on them for a lot of applications.

While many applications are complex, applications can also be simple. For example, a calculator is a common application on computers and devices, and it does some mathematical functions. Applications are the software programs that make computers so useful to use. The software program is written in code, but as users of the application we don't need to see the code because the software gives us menus, icons, and other ways to use the software to perform our work. Part of using software is the ability to translate, or interpret, instructions.

For a computer to use a software program, it has to be able to find and follow the instructions. This is what memory is used for on computers. The memory holds the instructions for the CPU to use. As the CPU follow the instructions of the software, it is moving information in and out of memory to perform the calculations.

Mobile devices like smartphones and tablets use software programs that are usually called "apps." An app is still an application, but since the devices started out smaller than computers, the term app was used and it seems to have stuck.

Operating Systems

While some software programs are applications, others types of software programs are called operating systems. An operating system is a software program that manages other software programs when they want to use the hardware. It's like a traffic cop at a busy intersection with a broken signal.

As cars approach the intersection, they are traveling a certain speed. Without a traffic cop, every car would drive into the intersection at the same speed it was approaching, and there would be collisions. The traffic cop manages how the cars can enter and use the intersection and sets up rules the cars have to follow in order to proceed through the intersection on their journey. How long one line of cars waits to use the intersection, who gets to make a left or right turn. And how fast they travel is all managed by the traffic cop.

An operating system, at it's most basic level, does the task of managing how other software programs use the hardware. An example is printing a document. When you want to print a document, the operating system manages when the processor can take care of printing. The operating system has to see what else is happening in the computer, stop any software program that needs to stop in order to print, then give the print job the resources to print.

The most common operating systems that you probably are familiar with are Microsoft Windows and Apple Mac OS. Mobile devices use operating systems also, and the two most popular mobile operating systems are Android and Apple's iOS. Operating systems make it easier for programmers to write software since they can write the software and not worry about the hardware. So as a result, software programs are said to be written for a specific operating system. The hardware, software programs (applications), and operating systems all work together.

It's common for computer companies to build everyday applications, like a web browser, into an operating system. As a result, you might not be aware of when you're using the operating system and when you're using an application. Many operating systems include applications, so the computer user is more likely to use the application already installed and included with the operating system, rather than adding and installing an independent programmer's version. As a result, many computer users assume that applications for common functions like email, photos, and web browsing are part of the operating system. But there's a balance that an operating system maker has to manage.

The line between an operating system and applications is sometimes blurry. Companies and organizations that make operating systems usually try to keep a balance between supplying applications for the convenience of their customers, but making it easy for application programmers to create and sell additional applications built to work with their operating system. This is important since people want to do things with their computers, and it's applications that make computers useful.

Software Programs and Operating Systems

One of the purposes of an operating system is to communicate and manage the hardware. A programmer's job is made easier by the operating system. Operating system software usually does common tasks, like printing a document or displaying graphics on a monitor. The operating system has programs that can talk to things like keyboards, printers, cameras, networks, and displays, so the programmer doesn't have to worry about writing "code" for their program to communicate with the hardware and do common tasks. And as hardware might be from different manufacturers or different models, having the operating system take care of the hardware offers more devices that can use the application.

An Apple iPhone, for example, uses Apple's iOS operating system. For any software program to work on an iPhone, it has to work with iOS since that's the only operating system on an iPhone. Apple uses the same operating system on all of it's iPhone models so a programmer can write an application that will work on different models of iPhones with one version of the software. The application is written to work with the operating system, and the operating system takes care of the differences in hardware.

Since software applications work with operating systems, it's important to know what operating systems a specific application with work with. A software program for Windows doesn't mean it will work on all versions of the Windows operating system. The software program is written to work with Windows 8, or 7, or Vista, or XP. Each one is a different operating system and a software program written for Windows 8 might not work on Windows Vista or XP.

Companies like Apple, Microsoft, and Google (who makes Android) know that while hardware is important, it's the applications that are the reason people buy a particular computer. As a result, good operating systems are important to attract more programmers to write applications.

What Are Software Updates and Upgrades?

Two terms that float around the computer world, sound similar, but have totally different meanings are "software update" and "software upgrade." You may even hear professionals incorrectly using the terms interchangeably, but there are important differences between the two that you should know.

Software update

An update is offered to you, free of charge, by the manufacturer of your original software. Manufacturers constantly monitor and improve their software programs to manage security issues that may come up over time. An update may also repair a problem that was discovered in the program code. A repair update is sometimes called a "patch." A patch replaces parts of the program to repair flaws while maintaining the integrity of the original program itself.

An update may improve a specific feature of the software, but if the software is not installed on your computer, you cannot update it. You are encouraged to download the update as soon as the manufacturer tells you it is available. The manufacturer does not want you to be using a flawed program that may have security issues.

For example, if you have Adobe Reader, you have probably noticed that you are asked frequently to update your program and it only takes a few seconds. Adobe constantly monitors it's program for security breaches, fixes them and provides updates to the software. You can only update Adobe if you have it installed on your computer.

Software upgrade

As opposed to the free software update, a software upgrade will cost you money. It is an entirely new improved version that totally replaces the older one. It's features are not just to get out the flaws or improve security but to provide an entirely new version with new basic features. You will need to install the entire software program the same way you do any new program.

Purchasing an upgrade is entirely optional and depends on the desires of the user. For example, Windows 8 is an upgrade to Windows 7. You may be very happy with your Windows 7 and, after reviewing the new improved features of Windows 8, decide you do not want or need it, so you do not purchase the upgrade. On the other hand, you may want the features of Windows 8. You purchase it from Microsoft and install it over Windows 7. You now have only the features of Windows 8.

What is a File Extension?

A File Extension is a short group of letters, occurring after the period in a file name, which indicates the format, function and identity of a given file of information.

The actual file name is the text used to the left of the period while the text to the right is the file extension. For example, if I wanted to save a file on my computer and call it "letter" I would be using the name "letter" as the name of my file. Let's take a look at how these two parts are used, then take a closer look at file extensions.

Why Do Computers Need File Extensions?

Even though I now have a file named "letter," there's something missing. Nothing in the name of the file tells my computer what type of information is in the file, or what type of software I would need to open, view, and use the file. If I add the extension ".doc" to the name of the file and call it "letter.doc" it has more meaning. The .doc extension is used to describe files that are created and used in word processing software. Now we know I have a document file. To open and edit the file I would need some type of word processing software on my computer.

So a very important role for file extensions is to help you, and your computer determine which programs can interact with different files. Your computer associates every type of file extension with a software application that can use that file extension. For instance, a file name with an extension of .xls would tell you the file is a spreadsheet that can be opened and edited with a spreadsheet program.

File Extensions and Specific Software Applications

You may have noticed that I didn't refer specifically to Microsoft Word when discussing a .doc file extension and instead referred to "word processing software" instead. This is because there are several software applications capable of using the .doc file extension. For example, you can open a .doc file using Apple's Pages application or the Google Docs application. So how is this possible?

Software applications often include tools to convert files from one file extension format to another. By converting the file, the software makes it possible to open and work with files created in a different application. If this wasn't available, it would be difficult to share files between people with different types of computers or different versions of software applications. Software companies usually make a point of letting you know in their description what types of files their software will work with, and this is a major selling point of them.

When opening a file, your computer looks at the file extension and then starts the software for opening files with that extension. Most software applications let your computer know what file extensions they are capable of working with. Your Web browser software (commonly Internet Explorer, Safari, Firefox, Chrome) is used to open Web pages with the .htm or .html file extension. You don't have to tell your computer what software to use with the .htm or .html extension since your Web browser software did that for you.

But in some cases, software might not have told your computer to use it for a specific file extension or you may not have the software needed to open a specific file extension. In this case you might see a message appear on your screen asking you to choose an application from a list. If you know what type of information is in the file by knowing a little about file extensions, you can them tell your computer what software it should use to open a specific file extension.

File Extensions are Used as Nouns

File extensions are often used as a noun, separate from any specific file name, to describe the type of information in a file. Written in the form of an abbreviation or acronym, the file extension is used as a format such as .doc, .xls, or .pdf, which are some common file extensions you may have already seen and used. It's also correct to use the file extension without the period. In this case the files are just referred to by the text used for the file extension, such as doc, xls, or pdf, and you might even see the extension used in all capital letters such as PDF. Regardless of the way they are used, the file extension refers to the type of information contained in the file and software required to open and use the file.

Knowing About File Extensions Can Help You

Even though there are thousands of different file extensions, it 's not necessary to learn them all. Usually your computer knows what software to use for specific file extensions. But if you can familiarize yourself with the most common file extensions, you can quickly learn how different files interact with different programs.

First, knowing the meaning of common file extensions can help you easily identify the type of information in a file. For instance, if you are searching for a group of images or pictures, you can search for image file extensions.

Examples of common extensions associated with images are JPG, GIF, and PNG. Additionally, if you are looking for an audio or song file, you can limit your search to files ending with WAV, MP3, FLAC, OGG and AIFF extensions.

As you become more familiar with different file extensions, you can learn which programs are compatible with different file types. Knowing that a video file might have a file extension such as .mp4 would make it easier to recognize that the file is a video. If you were looking for a video that's great, but if you were looking for files that were images you would know to skip over the video .mp4 files.

Knowing that a file contains a spreadsheet, such as a file with the XLS extension, can help you locate information quicker and save you time. You won't have to open the files to see what's inside if you understand the file extension when you see it.

The best way to learn about a file extension you don't recognize is to do an Internet search for the file extension name. This will usually reveal an explanation of the file extension and software that uses that extension. In case you want to view a list, here's a link to the Wikipedia list of file extensions.
http://en.wikipedia.org/wiki/List_of_file_formats_%28alphabetical%29

What's a JPEG, GIF, PNG, and PDF?

Have you ever seen a web page that asks "would you prefer to download you file as a jpeg, gif, or pdf file? If your next step is to pick one at random, read on and I'll try to explain some of these terms.

Photos, pictures, and other graphics can be used on computers, tablets, and smartphones because they are digital files. The information that is needed to display a photo or image on a screen is contained in the file, and converted into an image on your screen by software on your computer and device.

The jpeg, gif, and pdf terms tell both you and your Computing device how the image is stored and what software is necessary to Open and display the image file. The letters jpeg, gif, PDF, are all called file extensions and are used after the dot in a file name. computers read the file name and use the extension to decide what software should be used to open and disply the file.

For example, a file might be "image.jpeg" and your computer (or mobile device) will know it needs to use software that will open up and display a jpeg file on the screen.

If your computer has software to do that, it will display the image. Fortunately, computers and mobile devices have built-in software that will display the most common image file types.

Image files differ in whats called resolution, which is the amount of detail and data contained in the image file. Images used on web pages are meant for displaying on a display screen and don't need a great deal of resolution. They can be smaller and as a result, display faster when viewed on a web page. The jpeg and gif file are commonly used for images on web pages. You might also see a file called png which is becoming more common.

Your computer or mobile device uses its built in software to display these types of files. Jpeg, gif, and png files are compressed, meaning that not all of the data that was in the original image is contained in the compressed file. Graphic artists and web designers use software that compresses the original file, converting it to a jpeg, gif, or png file, making it smaller in size, and faster for displaying on the web.

What's a Virus, Worm, and Trojan Horse?

Virus, Worm, or Trojan Horse are terms used to describe different types of malicious software. If the word 'malicious" sounds bad, you're right, and you don't want any of these types of software on your computer.

Virus

A virus is a piece of software that installs itself on your computer and causes harm to your computer and data. With high-speed Internet connections, computers "catch" infections, most often when files are downloaded and as attachments to email. Viruses are created on a regular basis by computer hackers who sometimes use them as a challenge to see if they can get them to work or as a way to take control of a computer for some other purpose. Seldom do hackers have a constructive motive.

Running a current up-to-date anti-virus program will help prevent a virus from being installed by detecting any that appear in a file and sealing off the file to "quarantine" it, thereby sealing that file and preventing the virus from entering and contaminating your computer.

Before downloading any files, no matter what type, make sure you have anti-virus software installed and set to always be running so that it can do its job and protect you and your computer.

Worms

A Worm is another type of malicious software. A worm causes damage by copying itself over and over again to disrupt and eventually disable your computer.

Your anti-virus software typically checks for worms, which are also considered to be a specific type of virus.

Trojan Horse

A "Trojan horse" is named after the Greek legend. In this case, a malicious program is contained within a seemingly legitimate program. Just like in the Greek legend, malicious software is contained inside what looks to be a legitimate file, deceiving you, and potentially deceiving your anti-virus program.

What Can You Do?

Using and keeping your anti-virus software updated is critical for computer security and safety.

Microsoft Windows based computers, because they are the most commonly used, are also the most frequent target for malicious software. Windows XP, Vista, and Windows 7 all require additional anti-virus software. Microsoft now provides a free one, which I recommend in my classes, called Microsoft Security Essentials. Windows 8, Microsoft's newest operating system includes anti-virus software.

Apple's Mac computers include anti-virus and other security software in the operating system provided by Apple, so no additional software is necessary.

And last, mobile devices like iPhones, iPads, Android, Windows Mobile, and Blackberry RIM devices all include software from the manufacturer. All that's necessary for you to do is to update your device's software when the manufacturer provides one.

Networks and Connections

What is an IP Address?

An Internet Protocol Address, more commonly referred to as an IP address, is a unique number assigned to each device on the internet. Think of an IP address as a computer's home address.

Today there are literally billions of devices on the internet ranging from personal computers to smart phones and other connected devices. Together they form a complex network in which any device can communicate with any other device all thanks to their unique IP address.

Why Do Computers use IP Addresses?

Any computer or device connected to the Internet requires an IP address. The IP address is a unique number that allows other computers and devices to send information to any computer with an IP address.

Whenever a message (like an email) is sent from your computer, your computer's IP address is included in the message. You don't see this, and you don't need to worry about it. But any other computer or device on the Internet will know what IP address sent the message. So if it's necessary to send a reply back to your computer, any other computer will know to include your computer's IP address in the message so the Internet will deliver the message to your computer.

There are, however, many types of messages that are sent and received by computers when using the Internet. Often these include Web pages that are sent to your computer when you're browsing the Web, information you might use to fill out a form on a Web page, and files, like photos or documents, that you might download from a Web page or another computer on the Internet. Each of these actions uses the IP addresses of your computer and the other computer or device to make sure information is sent and received to the right location.

The easiest way to relate to something you are familiar with is how we use postal addresses to send physical mail and packages. When you prepare a label or address an envelope to be mailed, you're required to complete an address that tells the postal service where the item is to be delivered. The address is unique, meaning there is only one location that receives deliveries. While we use names, street numbers, cities, states, and postal codes, the Internet just replaces all of that with one number, the IP address.

When mailing an item, you also place your return address on the envelope or label. This is primarily used in case your item can't be delivered, and then the postal service returns it to the sender's address. Your computer's IP address is used for the same purpose. Just in case your message can't be delivered, the Internet will notify your computer that there was an error. If it's an email, you'll usually receive an email message telling you your email couldn't be delivered.

Why Don't We Need to Enter IP Addresses?

While computers are very good at numbers, people generally prefer a language, like English, Spanish, etc.. To make our lives easier, smart people that invented the Internet created a special software called Domain Name Servers, or DNS for short. Now you may have heard about DNS or something called a DNS server, but whether or not you have, here's what they do for you.
A DNS server is a computer that translates IP addresses to Domain Names and vice-versa. While Domain Names was

the topic of a different tech term newsletter, you use them all the time when browsing the Web and using email. When you address an email to someone, what comes after the @ symbol is the domain name. Common email domains are @gmail.com, @yahoo.com, @outlook.com, and you may have your own domain name for your own email. Web sites use the domain names as well, only with the www before the domain.

Domain Name Servers translate the domain name into an IP address, so messages addressed to a domain are delivered to the right computer on the Internet. Without DNS, we'd have to remember every Web site or domain by it's IP address. Trust me, domain names are easier to remember than IP addresses, so thank you to the people that invented DNS.

Sources and Types of IP Addresses

IP addresses are assigned by a special group called the Internet Assigned Numbers Authority, or IANA for short (http://www.iana.org). IANA is part of the Internet Corporation for Assigned Names and Numbers (http://www.icann.org) which is an international non-profit. This way, all IP addresses work the same all over the world, and the IANA is the source for all IP addresses. So who can get an IP address from them?

Organizations that run Internet operations, which include Internet Service Providers, Web hosting services, large corporations, schools, and governments are eligible to apply for a set of assigned IP addresses. The IANA reviews their request, and if approved, assigns a specific set of IP addresses which the organization can use in their operations. However, IP addresses can be assigned to a computer for temporary use or for permanent use.

Temporary IP Addresses

While the organization that has the use of the IP addresses can assign them to computers and other devices connected to the Internet, an address can be assigned for temporary use or for permanent use on a computer or device.

Temporary IP addresses, also referred to as "Dynamic IP Addresses," are IP addresses that are not assigned permanently to a specific computer or device. The IP address is "loaned" out for the computer or device to use while it's connected.

For home users, your Internet Service (usually your cable or phone company, but there are others), has the use of a block of IP addresses. When you connect to their network, they assign your computer a temporary IP address for your use. Although temporary, it's unique to your computer or device, and any computer on the Internet will know your address.

This temporary address is yours to use as long as you're connected to the Internet. Power off your computer, or disconnect your network connection, and you could be assigned a new IP address the next time you connect. Your computer knows how to make this work, and it allows Internet Service Providers a way to make much more efficient use of their block of assigned IP addresses.

Locations like coffee shops, hotels, libraries, and schools allow users to connect and assign a Dynamic IP Address since the computer or device is often connected for a short period of time.

In your home, your IP address may be assigned to each of your devices by the router provided by your Internet Service Provider. In this case, your router is assigned an IP address by your Internet Service when it connects to the

Internet. This is a Dynamic IP Address assigned by your ISP. Then your router assigns IP addresses to your computers and devices internally.

Private and Public Addresses

Your router uses a special range of IP addresses that are set aside specifically for this type of use, called Private IP Addresses. These Private IP address cannot connect to the Internet directly since the are not unique, and no computer on the Internet will be able to direct traffic to them. The advantage of using Public IP Addresses is that these IP addresses can be used over and over for any private network, since no two private networks ever connect with each other directly.

Your router uses a range of Private IP addresses that are part of the factory settings and assigns them one at a time to any computer or device, like a printer that connects to your home or small office network. The router uses the Public IP address assigned by your Internet Service to connect to the Internet. Internet devices only know your router's IP address, and it's up to the router to keep track of your local, Private IP addresses. By using Private IP addresses, it's possible to reuse the same set of IP address numbers for any Private Network. This makes it easier to setup a home or small business network since unique assigned IP addresses are not required.

Permanent or "Static" IP Addresses

Some computers and devices have a static IP addresses that never change. A static IP address is often required for certain functions on the Internet. It's used by computers that host Web sites, email services, remote backup sites, routers, and other network and computing devices.

Static IP addresses are used when it's important for a computer to have a permanent location that other computers can locate. For example, the computer for the home page of Yahoo! would be hard to find if it relied on a Dynamic IP address. By assigning a Static IP address, all the thousands of Domain Name Servers can remember Yahoo!'s location and quickly translate the domain name to the correct IP address.

Will You Ever See an IP Address?

Understanding a little about IP addresses helps you appreciate how sophisticated the Internet is. So often we take it for granted that when we type in a Web page address or click on a link in an email we receive the correct information on our desktop or mobile device.

If you just use the Internet for casual use, you may never see an IP address. When you connect to a WiFi network and are able to use it, you'll know that some device assigned an IP address to your computer, laptop, tablet, or smartphone so it can communicate with the Internet.

Tips for Solving Common IP Address Problems

Our homes and offices becoming more connected and dependent on the Internet. So knowing a little about IP addresses might help you solve some common problems with a network. Often, if the cause of the problem is with the IP addresses used by your computers or devices, it can help to power off everything, then power up everything. It's the first step that Internet Services usually tell home and small office users to do to solve network problems.

When powering every computer and network device off on your home network, you're setting them up so they will ask for a new IP address when they are powered on again. The first device to power on is your access device. Sometimes this is the router, but often it's just a box from your Internet Service that connects to them and has a single network connection. Powering this device off, then on, makes a new request from the device to your Internet

Service for a connection, including a new IP address (remember, these are Dynamic IP addresses your ISP assigns to you). You should wait a few minutes before powering up the next device on your network, your router.

Then you would power on your router. It takes about 3-4 minutes to "boot," since it's a computer, but one that's dedicated to being a router. Once your router is powered on, then you can power on your other computers, but do them one at a time. This way each one can request and receive it's IP address. It's a good idea to test each Internet connection as you power on the devices by seeing if you can open a Web page to view.

Network printers are sometimes powered off and powered on, and sometimes they change their IP address in the process. If the printer's IP address changed, your computer may not be able to find the printer again on the network. Sometimes just removing the printer from your computer's printer settings and adding it back in solves this problem. Newer printer models generally have features that make it easier to connect to a home or small office network.

While routers (which we covered in a previous newsletter) are reliable, sometimes replacing a router that's a few years old with a newer model can solve IP address and network problems. If your router is more than 3-4 years old, it might not have been designed for all the mobile and wireless devices available today. While your router may work for most devices, if you're having trouble connecting some devices to your home network, a $50-$75 dollar router replacement is often less expensive than hiring someone to come out and fix a problem, which might involve a router replacement anyway.

What are Mbps and Bandwidth?

Megabits per second is used to describe the speed at which digital data travels from one point to another. The capacity of a connection is referred to as it's bandwidth. Bandwidth is measured in bits per second and one Megabit per second is 1,000 bits per second. Mbps is commonly used to describe how fast a connection is from a computer, smartphone, tablet, or network to the Internet. The higher the Megabits per second, the faster data moves from one point to another.

A bit is a single unit of data used in digital computing. Moving bits from one point to another is important as more people use digital devices. Using email and the Web all involve moving data from one location to another, so the speed at which data can be moved is important.

The Digital Highway

You might have heard of the phrase "the digital highway," which is often used to describe the movement of data across the Internet. And in many ways, moving digital data is similar to how vehicles move on the road. If you think of freeways, there are different sizes, shapes, and capacities. How fast a single vehicle travels on the road depends on the capacity of the road (bandwidth) and how many other vehicles are using the same road. The bits that travel on the Internet are similar to our vehicle analogy.

The Internet is a shared highway, just like our roads and freeways. Some roads have more capacity than others, with more lanes, higher speed limits, and even express lanes. The more capacity the road has for traffic, the faster vehicles can move from one point to another.

Data moves across both wired and wireless "highways." Our smartphones use wireless cellular connections to reach a cell tower, then the tower uses a cable to transmit data over wired, or what are called "landline" connections. For your information, any connection that isn't wireless is sometimes called a landline. Since the Internet is a shared "highway," it's necessary to have on and off ramps, only these are data connections made with wires, cables, and antennas, not roads.

The paths that carry data communications connect to points where data can be sent in different directions, just like when two freeways intersect, at a stoplight, or a traffic circle. How fast data moves from one point to another is measured in bits per second, and connections are usually fast enough now that the million is added on, making it Megabits per second.

What Types of Physical Connections Are Used?

The speed of a data connection depends on both what it's made out of (the material used for the connection), and the speed allowed by the owner of the connection to the users. So let's talk about the types of materials that are used for connections.

I already mentioned wireless cellular connections, but in addition to the cellular networks there are microwave, laser, and satellite types of wireless connections. Often it's easier to install a wireless microwave or laser connection to connect two buildings to each other rather than running wire or cable. For areas with no cable or phone wires, satellites are often used for data connections. Another example is satellite TV which sends broadcasts to your home using a satellite network.

Wired networks are often copper wire or fiber-optic cable. Copper wire is used in Ethernet, telephone, and cable TV connections. Fiber-optic cable is often used in networks because it has the highest data transmission rate possible. Now, just because you have a cable or wireless connection that is capable of transmitting data really fast doesn't mean you always get fast data transmission. That part has to do with the way the owner of the path sells it.

How Mbps and Bandwidth are Sold

Someone paid for all these cell towers, satellites, microwaves, copper wire, and fiber optic cable installed, so somebody owns the paths. Ownership of a data path is more like a toll road than public highways. Somebody owns the road, either the government or a private company. And a toll is paid in order to drive on that path. Data paths are privately owned, usually by businesses, and they charge users to use the path, depending on how much data, and how fast a user wants to move their data.

Typically, a data path has more capacity than what just one customer might use. For example, a cable or wired connection from your home might be just yours to use. At some point several homes are connected to a single cable, sharing the capability of that path. That cable then connects with other groups of homes, until the connection reaches a central office. Even then, one very high-speed connection might carry all the data traffic for from one city to another.

Cell towers are another form of shared connection. One tower may supper dozens of users all making phone calls, using email, and browsing the Web. The cell tower is capable of supporting more than just one user at a time. Cell towers and cables get congested just like vehicle traffic, and when that happens the network can slow down. But it depends on whether a user has a "committed" bandwidth or not. Any user that has a committed amount of speed will be given priority over a user that has no commitment.

For most of our residential, cellular, and small business connections, there is no Mbps commitment from the provider, regardless if it's a phone, cable, or satellite company. If you read the fine print closely, you'll see that your Internet connection can be "up to" a certain Mbps. You may get that speed most of the time, but it's not a level of service that requires your provider to meet any minimum requirement.

The Internet provider allows enough speed (measured in Mbps) so the average customer doesn't notice when their connection might be a slower. Customers who need more bandwidth, because they need to move more bits or have more devices on their Internet connection, may notice that their Internet speed slows down. When this happens, your provider can add more capacity, like adding lanes to a freeway, but more often the provider offers an upgrade to a faster service for an additional fee. An upgrade to your Internet Mbps bandwidth is the equivalent of the freeway express lane, which requires a paid fee to travel in the higher speed traffic lane.

How Much Speed is Used?

If you have one computer in your home or business, even a 3-4 Mbps speed will allow you to watch Netflix on your Internet connection. But if you have more users in your home, you may need a faster connection since more users are sharing the available bandwidth speed. So a little math can help you figure this out.

Remember, a Mbps is one million bits per second. That means a file size of one megabit will take one second to move from the Internet to your computer. Text files, like emails and documents, are small files, they aren't usually larger than one Megabit, so email can move pretty fast even at one Mbps. A photo is a larger file, and some photos are larger than one Megabit, so many photos can take a little longer to travel. Two files that are one megabit each will take two seconds to travel on a one Megabit per second path. If the path is two Megabits per second, the files can travel in one second, since the path is 2x faster.

The average iTunes song is about 4 Megabits, so with a one Megabit per second path, it would take 4 seconds to download. Or to download a single song in one second, you would want a 4 Megabit per second connection. So your choices are to wait a little longer, or use (and pay) for a faster connection. If you have 3 people using a shared Internet connection, they all share the available bandwidth. So the one Megabit per second path we're using an example here is shared by all three users.

People and their devices are only using the bandwidth when they are actually sending or receiving data. So for a Web page, once the Web page is received on a user's computer or smartphone, their use of the bandwidth stops, until they click on another link and request a new Web page. Someone may be reading email, but they aren't using the bandwidth until they send and receive new mail messages.

If everyone wants to send and receive data at the same time, the path gets "congested" and reaches it's capacity limit, and everyone's data bandwidth slows down. If this is happening to you and you want a faster connection, you'll have to upgrade with your service provider.

A Little Perspective

At one time bandwidth was measured in kilobits per second, or Kbps. A kilobit is 1,000 bits, and a megabit is 1,000 kilobits, so a Mbps is 1,000 times faster. And a gigabit is 1,000 megabits, so one Gbps is 1,000 times faster than a one Mbps connection.

In the section on ISP's there's a link to a website and a mobile app for testing your Internet connection speed.

What is an ISP?

ISP stands for Internet Service Provider. In short, an Internet Service Provider is a company in the business of connecting people to the Internet. You, as the computer user, pay a fee to the ISP and in return, they connect your computer (or computers) to the Internet. Phone companies, cable companies, cellular providers, and other telecommunications companies are usually the businesses that provide Internet connections. They may offer additional services, but we're talking about them being your ISP right now. Familiar ISPs are often your local cable company, phone company or satellite television company, and with names like AT&T, Verizon, Time-Warner, COX, Charter, etc.. There are many independent ISP's also, and some common names are Earthlink and NetZero.

The Internet Utility

If you think of the Internet as a utility like water, electricity, or gas, there are many similarities between ISP's and these utilities. ISP's provide the Internet access by purchasing access to the Internet in large amounts of capacity, then break it down into smaller amounts for home and business use. Internet access is similar to the electricity, gas, and water that's used by a utility. The Internet comes to your home, business, or mobile devices in the data that's contained in Web pages, emails, and other files. ISP's, just like utilities, have to have ways to get the Internet data to and from their customers. This is the distribution system, and it's often referred to as the "pipes" of the Internet as a slang term by techies. Internet speeds are determined by the type and capacity of the connection to the ISP. So what are they?

Internet Capacity

Depending on the speed of your service and your ISP, you might connect with a dial up phone connection, a wireless connection, a satellite connection, a cable connection, or a fiber optic connection. Dial up is the slowest of these, while fiber is the fastest possible connection. Internet pipes can be slow if they can only handle moving a certain amount of data, just like a water or gas pipe is slow if it can only handle a certain amount of liquid or gas. Larger pipes, with larger capacity, can move water and gas faster, and so can larger pipes for the Internet. However, just like a water or gas pipe, you don't have to use all the capacity that's available. How much capacity you have to your home or business depends on how much capacity you purchase. So how does pricing affect what an ISP does?

Internet Pricing

Internet connections from ISP's are usually priced similar to each other. After all, the Internet isn't different from one ISP to another, it's access and capacity you're paying for with the ISP. One ISP can't offer you access to a different part of the Internet than another ISP, so pricing is very competitive. Each ISP will have a different cost structure based on your location in the country, the kind of connection you want to establish and how much you plan on accessing the Internet. So how do they vary in price?

ISP Differences and Services

ISP's offer different pricing based on the amount of data you want receive and send when using the Internet, and with a variety of additional services. For home connections, we usually want fast downloads since most of our home activity is receiving data from the Internet on our computers. This includes watching movies, playing music, and browsing the Web. As a result, most home ISP's offer a fast download, but a slower upload, since we don't really need to send much information to the Internet as home users. Business, academic, and professional users often need to both receive and send larger amounts of data than home users, and pricing is usually higher for faster upload and download speeds. So basically, the more capacity you use, the more you pay, just like more water, gas, or electricity on your utility bills.

Some ISP's offer different types of services and support and their prices vary. For example, if you wanted priority support 24 hours a day, you would probably have to pay for a more expensive service. If you wanted email accounts from your ISP, one might be free, but additional emails might cost more.

How to Choose?

The decision on which ISP to choose has a lot to do with your Internet habits and how quickly you need the Internet to respond. Unless you have many computers or wireless devices like tablets or smartphones in your home, the basic ISP services will likely be more than enough for what you need. If you have a family that uses the Internet for watching movies has a lot of devices, or you have a small business, you might want to look into upgraded services.

Testing Your Internet Speed

ISP's use speed testing tools and monitor your capacity and can often tell how much capacity you are using and need by contacting technical support. There is a Web site at www.speedtest.net and an app for smartphones called SpeedTest that can test your connection speed and show you what your download and upload speeds are. If your curious, check them out. With cellular phones, connection speeds can vary greatly based on your location, cellular provider, and phone capability, while home and business connections tend to be more consistent since they use wired connections to the ISP.

In the alphabet soup that is the tech industry, knowing what an ISP is and what it can do for you will give you a leg up in making decisions about how you interact and connect to the Internet.

Wireless Networking

Wireless networking does exactly what it says. It takes the physical wires out of the picture and uses wireless technologies to replace the wires. Wireless communication has made mobile computing possible since devices can connect to each other and the Internet without the need for a cable connection.

There are multiple types of wireless technologies and each one has it's own features and benefits. So let's learn more about them and how they work. Once we cover these, we'll go on to mobile devices.

What is WiFi?

WiFi commonly refers to a wireless connection to the Internet. A WiFi connection to the Internet uses a wireless signal to transmit and receive Internet data between one or more computers or other devices such as a tablet or smartphone.

What Does WiFi Mean?

The term WiFi comes from the acronym for two words, wireless and fidelity. Wireless refers to the fact that an Internet signal is obtained without using direct wiring or cables. Like any wireless signal, an antenna is used to transmit and receive the WiFi signal. Your computer, tablet, smartphone, game console, TV, or other device needs a WiFi antenna to transmit and receive WiFi data. You may not see the antenna on the outside of your device, but if your device works with WiFi, it has a built-in antenna.

The Fidelity Part of WiFi

The second word of the acronym Wi-Fi is a bit more obtuse. Fi comes from the word Fidelity. This is a term that was previously used extensively in the business of recording and playback of music. Before there were computers, music was played on phonographs that picked up sound from a record. Early records had questionable quality and poor sound quality, or fidelity. Fidelity means the sound is as faithfully reproduced as current technology allows.

As records and phonographs improved, advertisers denoted some records and phonographs as High Fidelity. Thus, application of the term fidelity, as part of the acronym Wi-Fi, is accomplished by using the letters "Fi." So now that we know where the term WiFi came from, how does it work?

Using WiFi to Access the Internet

Your WiFi computer or device connects to another WiFi device, which is almost always a router. Routers are a specialized computer which does routing of data on networks. Most home and small business routers have a built-in WiFi antenna and if they have this antenna, they have WiFi capability. The router also has a wired connection to the Internet, usually to your Internet Service Provider (often your cable or phone company).

The router's antenna broadcasts a WiFi signal so your devices can locate it. For two devices to use WiFi, they need to recognize each other. WiFi networks use what's called a "handshake" before two devices can send and receive data to each other. It's like introducing two people to each other so they can start a conversation. Handshakes vary from one WiFi network to another since some don't require a password and some do, depending on how the WiFi network is set up to work.

Once your device has been introduced to the router and is on to the WiFi network using the "handshake," it can send and receive data using WiFi. The router communicates with devices connected to it using WiFi, using the WiFi side of the network. It then connects the WiFi side of the network to the Internet using the router's wired connection to your Internet Service Provider.

WiFi is a Radio Signal

WiFi networks commonly use one of two radio frequencies, 2.4Ghz and 5Ghz. These are radio frequencies managed in the U.S. by the Federal Communications Commission and around the world by the respective country's regulations.

Since WiFi uses radio signals, it can vary in signal strength based on distance, obstructions, and interference. These can all affect the reliability and speed of your WiFi Internet connection. Distance can affect your WiFi signal strength as you move further away from the antenna on your WiFi router. While many WiFi routers will broadcast a signal to most of a home, sometimes the distance is so far that the signal becomes too weak to use and you lose your Internet connection in certain locations.

This is why you can sometimes pick up the signal of your neighbor's WiFi router on one side of your home, although you would need a password to connect to it. If your signal is too weak in parts of your home, see if you can move your router to a location closer to the center. If not, you can add a router and cable to rebroadcast the signal to a new area of your home. This is how offices and schools create a signal that seems like it's available everywhere.

WiFi is a World Standard (for more techie types to read)

An international standards body called the Institute of Electrical and Electronics Engineers (IEEE) created the WiFi standard in 1997 and publishes the technical specifications so any manufacturer can build devices using the WiFi standard. The common term for the WiFi standard used for networks is called 802.11, and you may see this number on WiFi devices. The number comes from the group number at the IEEE that manages the standard. Technology companies, research organizations, and other organizations have volunteer IEEE members that serve on these standards groups.

Different WiFi Standards

As WiFi has developed, standards for it have changed to provide increased range and data. To tell what version of the standard your device uses, you'll need to know the number and letter of the WiFi standard it uses. These numbers all begin with 802.11, which is named after the IEEE group that manages the WiFi standard.

The 802.11 number will also have a letter after it, such as 802.11b, 802.11g, and 802.11n. As long as the two devices you want to connect to each other using WiFi have the same WiFi capability, they can connect with each other. Almost every device manufactured today includes support for 802.11b and 802.11g, so they will work with each other. Newer and higher priced routers may also include support for the latest version of the standard, 802.11n. The problem with 802.11n is that the standard isn't quite completed, so it's possible that two devices made by different manufacturers may not work together. However, all 802.11n routers also include support for 802.11b and 802.11g so they support almost every WiFi device made.

Technology Changes

As technology changes, updating one part of your technology may create issues with other parts. Our homes are becoming pretty sophisticated with desktops, laptops, tablets, smartphones, Internet TV, game consoles, and other Internet connected devices coming out like thermostats and light controls. As a result, it's sometimes necessary to upgrade an older part of your technology in order to work with something new. Often this is the case with WiFi.

If you have an older router, it may have problems connecting with newer devices like tablets, so often a router replacement which is usually under $100, will fix connection issues.

Often replacing technology is an easier, lower cost, and faster solution to trying to repair or fix a problem.

What is a HotSpot?

From coffee shops to train stations and airports, you may have noticed the increasing visibility of signs indicating that these places are hotspots. No, that doesn't mean there is volcanic activity brewing beneath your local coffee shop. A hotspot is simply an area with wireless Internet access. No one is sure just where the term hotspot started being used, but the best guess is that the Finnish cellular company, Nokia, may have been responsible for creating the term.

Hotspots can be thought of as a local area within which people can connect to the Internet wirelessly. A hotspot is created when a wireless router is connected to the broader Internet. The router generates a Wi-Fi (wireless Internet) signal, which creates an area where other devices can receive the hotspot signal. Any person with a computer or other Wi-Fi enabled device can then connect to the hotspot. In other words, hotspots are areas where you can connect to the Internet without having to use cables or other physical connections.

Hotspots afford customers and clients an opportunity to access the Internet while doing everyday activities like studying for tests or fueling their cars. For instance, you may have noticed men and women working on their computers while drinking a cup of coffee; they are likely connected to the Internet within a hotspot. And this is the greatest benefit of hotspots: they provide individuals additional ability to multitask. Instead of having to choose work or play, you can do both, completing tasks while enjoying yourself in a non-office environment. Conversely, you can simply surf the web while doing a necessary chore. Common hotspot locations include restaurants, hotels, hospitals, airports, bookstores, grocery stores, libraries, and schools. Some cities have even gone wireless with public wireless networks!

An individual can use a device that contains a wireless connection, like a laptop or phone, in a hotspot. Smartphones and mobile hotspot devices sold by cellular companies can create what are known as "personal hotspots." Using the cellular networks that these smartphones and devices use to connect to the Internet using their cellular data capability, they can use their WiFi capability to create a personal hotspot to connect nearby devices to the Internet. Personal hotspots are especially useful for travelers and others who might want to connect multiple items to the Internet in an easy and affordable fashion. For example, if you had a laptop or tablet that only had WiFi Internet capability, you couldn't connect to the Internet unless you could connect to a WiFi hotspot.

Use of Wi-Fi in a hotspot isn't always free. While establishments are increasingly offering Wi-Fi services free of charge, others only provide it at a price. You may have to enter credit card information as you log-on to wireless service, so be sure to confirm whether it's free or not if you want to avoid charges. Some hotspots aren't available to the public and may be locked, allowing only those individuals who have the password the ability to use the hotspot. If you have a wireless router in your home, your hotspot probably requires a password to use the Internet, which makes it a private hotspot.

Since hotspots are so widely available, using the Internet and working without a cable connection is easier all the time. So the next time you see a hotspot sign, take it as an invitation. Open up your tablet, phone, or laptop, and do more.

What Does 4G LTE Mean?

For most people, it can be confusing knowing exactly what 4G LTE means. Many purchase the latest smartphone without knowing what some of its features entail.

LTE Meaning

LTE is the acronym for Long Term Evolution and is used by ATT and Verizon Wireless to deliver data speeds that are significantly faster than 3G. 4G LTE is still being developed by the majority of wireless carriers and is useful in enabling certain processes to take place faster, such as streaming media, surfing the Internet and downloading content.

4G LTE Versus 4G

There is a difference between 4G LTE and 4G alone. For instance, the 4G HSPA+ network that T-Mobile currently offers is considerably faster than 3G and is deemed as "4G" although it is really closer to 3.5G. 4G LTE, on the other hand, is essentially up to 10 times faster than standard 3G. Everything takes place faster, from watching movies, to downloading apps, to uploading content on social media websites to loading a page on the Internet. The "G" in 3G and 4G is often the subject of confusion as well. "G" stands for "generation," which means that 3G is third generation and 4G fourth. It merely relates to the time frame when the network speeds were introduced to the wireless community. Every time a new generation of wireless network speeds is introduced, it is faster than the one before it.

4G LTE Availability

Generally speaking, 4G LTE is currently only offered in certain cities. It is still being developed by major wireless carriers and prepaid networks alike. In areas where it is not available, the individual will experience 3G speeds instead.

Mobile

What is a Smartphone?

A recent survey* showed that 88% of all adults over the age of 18 in the U.S. have a cell phone. One of the more complex and often mind-boggling decisions the non-tech-savvy person is confronted with is understanding the differences and choosing among the many mobile phones on the market now. It seems as though everyone should want a Smartphone, but is the opposite of a Smartphone a dumb phone? Let's try to break this tech term down into something understandable.

First, of course, is the basic cell phone. It's the least expensive to buy and usually the simplest to operate. It also offers the fewest functions, and as a result costs the least to use. Its user can make and receive phone calls, and virtually all basic phones can send and receive text messages. For some people, this is all they need.

What is a Feature Phone?

A feature phone is more technologically advanced than a basic cell phone and shares some similar characteristics with a smartphone, although it doesn't have as many features. It may allow you to download music and basic games, but you will not have the same Internet capabilities because they often connect only to slower Internet networks (GPRS or General Packet Radio Service), which is the slower compared to the 3G, 4G and WiFi connections that Smartphones use. If you have only GPRS on your feature phone, often you will only have access to the specific features (which is where the name feature phone comes from) your wireless carrier allows, such as news and weather. The features that are available can vary considerably from one phone or manufacturer's product to the next, which means that if you're considering acquiring one of these, you'll probably want to carefully research and compare which phones offer what features.

What is a Smartphone?

A smartphone is the high end among cell phones on the market today, and is truly a computer in your hand. This phone will have many capabilities that regular cell phones and feature phones lack. It often includes a touchscreen, used for navigation and starting "apps," which are like applications on a computer, only made for using on a smartphone.

A touchscreen keyboard is common on most smartphones, but some smartphones may have a physical keyboard with buttons for the keys, so a touchscreen is not the only thing that makes a phone a smartphone. Most people think of Apple iPhones and Android phones as the only smartphones, since they make up almost 90% of all smartphones sold today. There are others though. The Blackberry is considered a smartphone, and there are new Windows smartphones on the market now as well. They are all made for using with the Internet.

Compared to any other type of phone, smartphones also have powerful Internet capabilities, which is limited in feature phones and not used in most basic phones. To use the Internet, smartphones connect to the wireless carrier at the fastest speeds possible, using 3G or 4G LTE, which allows you to download data like music, email, watch videos, and surf the web just as you would do on a computer.

A smartphone also includes the ability to download and install apps from a third-party or manufacturer's marketplace, which allows you to add apps to your smartphone beyond the apps that were included with it. Smartphones, because they are really computers with a phone app, have faster processors (also known as CPU's) and more memory for storing apps, data, documents, games, photos, and other information.

Poll source: Pew Internet

What is Android?

If you are at all familiar with smartphones, you no doubt have heard the term "Android" plenty of times. However, if you are not all that tech savvy, you may wonder exactly what it refers to.

Android is an operating system designed for use on mobile devices like smartphones and tablets. It was developed by a company called Android, which was purchased by Google in July of 2005. With more people using mobile devices for accessing the Internet, Google certainly made a pretty smart decision.

Android Plays Nice With Others

An important aspect of Android is that Google allows and encourages other companies to use Android in their products. This process is called licensing, and when you purchase a smartphone or tablet with Android, the manufacturer has obtained a license from Google to install it on their device. This means that the operating system can be found on phones and tablets made by Samsung, LG, HTC, Sony and other manufacturers.

Google's licensing of Android also allows manufacturers to customize the look of their smartphone or tablet with a unique design. As a result, while all Android devices use the Android operating system, each one can be a little different based on the customization the manufacturer did for their device.

Like any software product, Android is updated regularly. Google uses both numbers and names for their versions of

Android, using a dessert or candy for each major version. The current version is the 4.2 Jelly Bean operating system, and 5.0 Key Lime Pie is expected to be released later this year.

Google also runs a few Web sites and services that just happen to work well with Android devices. Services you like gmail and Google Calendar are easy to setup and use with an Android device. And Google has it's own cloud storage and apps for documents, spreadsheets, and presentations. So for anyone already using Google services, Android is a very nice fit.

Not all Android devices use the same version of Android since the choice of which version to use is up to the manufacturer. As a result, the smartphones and tablets using the most recent version of Android, have all the newest features. But the devices using older versions of Android are limited to the features available in the Android version used on the device.

Keep this in mind if you're considering an Android device. Be sure to check to see what version of Android is uses, and if it can be updated, because some devices don't support updates. Often the free or less expensive devices cost less because they use older versions of Android.
Apps for Android
The ability of manufacturers to customize and choose which version of Android they use on a device has made Android the world's most popular mobile operating system for smartphones.

As a result, Android apps are readily available and there now almost as many apps available for Android as there are for Apple's iOS operating system.

Google runs an app marketplace called Google Play, where Android owners can browse and purchase apps, but

Google also allows others to sell apps for Android devices. Amazon, which uses a version of Android in their Kindle Fire product, has an app marketplace, and several cellular providers run their own app marketplaces.

Is Android Right for You?

With Android being a very capable mobile operating system you now have more competition and choice, which is good for the consumer. Some of your choices to change from one mobile operating system to another will have more to do with the content and apps rather than the device itself. If you have a lot invested in music, apps, or other content you've purchased for an iPhone, you'll have to replace all of that investment, with the possible exception of music. If you like using iTunes on your computer, or have been an iPod user, then an Apple device is probably the way to go since you're already familiar with Apple products.

If you are going to use a mobile device for email, messaging, social networks, taking pictures, or browsing the Web, and don't need the hand-holding support available from Apple, then Android is a good solution, as many have discovered.
For tablets, however, Android still lags behind Apple in the number of apps specifically built for the iPad, and the content available for movies, TV, and other media on Apple is second to none, which is why iPads still are the leading tablet sold worldwide.

What is a Touchscreen?

A touchscreen is a display surface that can interpret when something (usually a person's finger) touches it's surface. The act of touching the screen produces an electrical signal. This signal can be used just like a press of a key on a keyboard or a click of a mouse button. A touchscreen is different from other touch sensitive surfaces because it also includes a visual display that can display graphics and text.

Touchscreen Basics

Touchscreens have become the standard on smartphones and tablets and are also appearing in many other uses. Touchscreens offer greater versatility in product design by eliminating the need for a keyboard, mouse, and physical buttons. What makes touchscreens so versatile is not only the ability to respond to a touch, but to change the visual display that appears on the touchscreen surface.

If you've ever used a touchscreen device, you are already familiar with the fact that when you make contact with the touchscreen, your device reacts in some way. Your device might dial a phone number, change the visual display to show you new options, make a sound, snap a picture, or send an email. All of these are actions that occur as a result of some contact you made with the touchscreen. Your device's computer and software interpreted the contact you made with the touchscreen. You are using the touchscreen to send commands to your device using what are called "gestures."

Gestures

The software that runs on your device can interpret different ways you make contact with your touchscreen. What do I mean by contact? Human hands a pretty versatile and flexible and there are a couple of ways touchscreen engineers have figured out to take advantage of this. For example, a Tap is a common gesture on all touchscreen devices. It's used to start an app or give a command and it's similar to pressing a button. Did you ever wonder how your device knows it's a Tap? If so, read on.

Touchscreens can interpret where you make contact with the touchscreen. So if a button or command is in a particular position, the touchscreen will know that you are making contact in the location of a specific button. When you tap on a touchscreen keyboard, you are making contact with a specific character that you want to enter. I know that sometimes keyboards seem small on touchscreens, so you tap the wrong character and touchscreens are very sensitive about the position you made contact with it.

Your touchscreen can also interpret the duration of the contact you make with it, along with how many fingers you use, and if you move them while you are making contact with the touchscreen. So when you press your finger on the touchscreen and don't let go, your touchscreen knows that you are doing something different than a tap because of the amount of time you hold your finger on the touchscreen. Move your finger while touching it and you have what's called a "swipe."

All of these gestures are commands, and some gestures include using two fingers to "pinch" or "spread," which is how you can zoom in and out on web pages and maps. The touchscreen and software that interprets the gestures are able to give you a lot of control using just your hands. This eliminates the need for a bulky keyboard and mouse so you can use just the surface of your device to issues your commands. Touchscreens have made mobile computing possible by making smartphones and tablets self-contained devices.

How do they Display Information and Graphics?

Touchscreens are made in several layers of materials, that when manufactured, appear to be one solid surface. Most devices have a top protective layer to prevent scratches and damage. Beneath this is the touch sensing layer and beneath this layer is the display layer. The actual manufacture is much more complex and can include many more layers, but this is the basics.

These layers are all clear, except for the display layer at the bottom which is similar to what's inside the flat LCD (Liquid Crystal Display) computer display screen you might have for your computer. When your device is asleep, the screen display is off and doesn't respond to touchscreen gestures. That's why it's usually necessary to press a real physical button to wake up your device. Once your device is awake, the touchscreen is powered and is able to respond to your gestures.

Smartphone and tablet touchscreens respond to a light touch, but they aren't the only type of touchscreens. There are several types of touchscreens, which we'll learn about next.

Different Types of Touchscreens

There are two general types of touchscreens, ones that respond electrically, and ones that respond to pressure. And there are different touch options for them as well.

The common smartphone and tablet touchscreens respond to an electrical contact, and are called capacitive touch. Because the human body conducts electricity, when a finger makes contact with an electrically sensitive surface, a touchscreen can sense where your finger touched the screen. Capacitive touchscreens are very sensitive to touch and only require a light contact. Capacitive touchscreens don't work with non-conducting materials. This is why a ball-point pen doesn't work, and why there are stylus pens made with with conductive tips.

Capacitive touchscreens for smartphone and tablets are also referred to as "multi-touch." This means that they sense the duration and number of fingers when contact is made. While multi-touch screens respond to the widest variety of touch, there are touchscreens made that respond to a single touch and some that respond to two touch points. These are generally less expensive than the multi-touch type and are used in retail point of sale and industrial applications where multi-touch isn't required for the touchscreen.

The other general type of touchscreen is resistive touch. If you've ever used a card swiper at a checkout register at a retail store or a car GPS screen, you've probably used a resistive touchscreen. These types of screens are made with layers, but a touch occurs when pressure is applied at a point, creating electrical contact between two layers. This is just like pressing a physical button, but the visual display can change, and you can press any button created by the display.

Because resistive touchscreens use pressure, the surface is not the smooth clear glass you see on a capacitive touchscreen, but usually a frosted clear surface. Because resistive touchscreens don't use glass for their surface, they less likely to break or shatter so they are used for retail and other public locations.

What's Next?

Touchscreens have become so widely used for mobile computing devices that other types of technology are starting to use them. Microsoft's Windows 8 Operating System was designed from the ground up to work with a touchscreen computer display. Apple's Magic Mouse and Touchpad are touch sensitive devices made for people who want to use gestures to control their computer or laptop. In the future, we'll see more devices using touchscreens   that use buttons and keys.

What is Bluetooth?

Bluetooth is a wireless communication standard that connects electronic devices to each other. If you're wondering what those things are that resemble large hearing aids in so many people's ears, those are Bluetooth receivers. The receiver communicates with a cell phone using Bluetooth.

Bluetooth creates a great way to communicate between an automobile, a computer, or an earpiece, to a cellular phone. It's a high tech, wireless way to exchange digital or voice data over a short distance, which is 10 meters, or about 32 feet.

The Reason Bluetooth Exists

Bluetooth was originally invented for use with cell phones. A wireless communications technology was needed that wouldn't use much of the battery power in a cell phone, could be used in very small devices, like earpieces, and was as low cost as using a cable connection. Lower power, however, translates into low range, and that's why there's a limit of 10 meters, which is about 32 feet.

Bluetooth was invented by Dr. Jaap Haartsen while he worked at Ericsson, the Swedish electronics company. The name Bluetooth is from a 10th century Danish king, Harald Blåtann Gormsson. According to legend, Harald was well known for getting different tribes to communicate with each other. He also had a love of blueberries, which stained his teeth, and was nicknamed King Blåtann, which translates into English as "Bluetooth." The Bluetooth logo consists of the Nordic runes for his initials, H and B (since my wife is Norwegian this has to be mentioned in the article).

One advantage of Bluetooth is that it's a worldwide industry standard, and it is a low-cost, easy to manufacture technology. As a result, there are an estimated 2 billion

Bluetooth devices in use around the world made by over 17,000 companies that are members of the Bluetooth. To use Bluetooth with a device, who belong to the Bluetooth Special Interest Group, which oversees the qualifications and specifications of Bluetooth devices, and protects the Bluetooth trademark. In order to manufacture and sell a piece of Bluetooth equipment, the device must meet the standards set by this group.

Bluetooth devices are always looking for another Bluetooth device that's nearby. They broadcast a signal that searches for any other Bluetooth device nearby, a lot like when kids yell "Marco" when they are playing Marco-Polo with each other. When another device answers "Polo," the two devices are ready to be connected. Connecting Bluetooth devices is done using a technique known as "pairing," which is like introducing one person to another by name. Once the two Bluetooth devices learn each other's "names," they become paired, and will automatically connect when they are within the range of each other. This is how your Bluetooth headset automatically connects to your cell phone when it's within the range of your cell phone, and how your cell phone will automatically connect up to your car's hands-free connection when you start your car. The requirement for pairing creates a secure connection and keeps Bluetooth devices that are strangers from communicating with any of your devices.

Some Bluetooth Examples

Bluetooth is a great technology for our mobile world, where so many devices rely on battery power. In addition to earpieces, there are Bluetooth keyboards for use with tablets, and Bluetooth speakers for tablets and smartphones. New Bluetooth devices are being introduced frequently, and with some creative uses. There's a Bluetooth scale that uses Bluetooth to send your weight to a smartphone app that keeps track of your weigh-ins, and a grill thermometer that displays the temperature of your steak on your smartphone as it cooks on the grill.

What is GPS?

GPS stands for global positioning system. The system is composed of 24 satellites that are constantly orbiting the earth from 1200 miles above it. Originally launched in 1978 by the U.S. Department of Defense, the satellite system was opened up for civilian use in the 1980s. The satellites constantly transmit information and run on solar energy.

Although the government does not charge for use of the system, you must purchase a receiver in order to access the system. The receiver is the GPS device that is sold and that you need to use in your car, boat or other vehicle. Many cellular phones, for example, iPhones and Android models, have built-in GPS receivers. The GPS receiver accesses the data transmitted from the satellites and interprets it in order to identify your location.

How a GPS receiver works.

It may seem like magic, but the GPS receiver is really a computer with software that calculates the data it receives from the satellites into information you can use. It needs to receive data from three satellites in order to identify your exact location.

You then enter your destination address. GPS software includes a map database that converts your location provided by the satellites, and the destination address you have entered, into a map that shows you the most direct route to your destination. It also includes the distance and travel time. Some other examples of GPS map databases are golf course GPS devices, which have golf course maps stored in their database, and hiking GPS devices, which contain a hiking trail database.

Some GPS receivers have an additional capability and can connect to the Internet. Usually this is through a cell phone network like Verizon, AT&T, or Sprint. Smartphones like the iPhone and Android models include this capability, and other GPS receivers are available with the ability to connect to the Internet. Using their Internet connection, these devices can access information that's available on Internet databases, such as real-time traffic information, and show it on their display screen.

Why some receivers are more expensive.

The cost of the receiver depends on the software included. You can add software that can locate and map specific locations. For example, you can get directions to the nearest Starbucks or gas station. You can buy one without a screen that tells you what to do by audio, or one with a screen so you can follow your progress on the map. The cost depends on the software you want included and the size of the screen.

The receiver needs a good antenna in order to receive the data from the satellites. Because the transmissions from the satellites travel by line of sight, the receiver does not work in caves, buildings, underwater or in tunnels.

Benefits of a GPS receiver.

The system works in all types of weather and works 24 hours a day. It will tell you exactly how to get to your destination from your current location, how long it will take you to there and how many miles away it is. If you use a GPS receiver, you may never get lost again.

What is a SIM Card?

A SIM card, or Subscriber Identity Module, is a small plastic memory card that is used in GSM cell phones. GSM stands for "Global System for Mobile Communications" and refers to the type of technology that is used by AT&T

and T-Mobile in the United States and in wireless carriers abroad. A SIM card is a necessary part in the operation of your cell phone. It fits inside a slot (usually along the phone's edge) of a mobile phone and contains personal information about the phone's owner. The card must be inserted into the cell phone's SIM slot in a specific position so that the data stored on it can be read by the phone.

There are now three different sizes of SIM cards available on the market. You can get a standard one that is often referred to as a mini-SIM. This is the largest type of SIM card that is used today. Many smartphones now use a micro-SIM, which is considerably smaller. The first phone known to take this type of SIM card was the iPhone 4, released by Apple in 2010. The newest type of SIM is the nano-SIM card, which is used in the brand new iPhone 5. The three are not interchangeable; you use the SIM card that fits your cell phone.

All SIM cards have gold strips on their undersides that is most likely made from tin or copper. These strips are essentially where all of your personal information is contained ~ items such as your phone number, service provider name (SPN), contacts, text messages and various other data. All SIM cards are internationally identified by what is known as an integrated circuit card identifier (ICCID) and contain a specific serial number.

The SIM card can be extremely useful. For example, if you frequently travel internationally, you can use your own phone if it is carrier- or factory-unlocked during your travels. The only requirement is that you purchase a prepaid plan with a SIM card at your destination and pop that SIM into your phone. Then, when you return home, you can go back to your regular SIM card and use your device locally.

World Wide Web

What is a URL?

URL stands for uniform resource locator. It's a text string of letters, numbers, and symbols that identifies a webpage, program, document, photo, or other resource found online.

How URLs Work

That didn't help much, right? Let's make it simpler. Imagine that you own a bakery. You want people to buy their bread from your bakery, but they have no idea where it's located. What can you do? Tell them your bakery's address, of course. Whenever they want to visit your bakery, they can just get in a cab and give the address to the driver. In turn, the driver will be the one to find the way and drop them off at their destination.

Now, let's say you have a website called Bobology. This website is out there on the Internet, just waiting to be visited. But aside from you, no one else knows where it is is, so it's in danger of getting lost amid the millions of other websites online. What can you do? Tell people your website's URL, which is http://www.bobology.com. This is what people type in the address bar of the browser they're using.

So in the above scenario, the URL is like the bakery's address, the address bar of the browser is like the cab, and the computer is like the driver. If you imagine it that way, it's easy to see how a URL functions. Interestingly, a URL is sometimes called Web address, which gives our analogy more sense.

A URL has three parts:

1. The URL protocol — These are the letters preceding the characters :// The URL protocol most people are familiar

with is http://, which is used for websites. The http stands for HyperTest Transport Protocol, which helps the computers that run Internet understand how to send and receive information.

2. The address itself (or host name) — This is a name that separates a website from all the others. It should be a unique name. For Bobology, it's http://www.bobology.com. The www after the http:// stands for World Wide Web, which is used by the Internet computers to determine that the address is located on the World Wide Web, which is the Internet.

3. The location of the file or resource — A URL can lead to a specific location within a website. For example, the URL http://www.bobology.com/public/Bobology-Blog-by-Bob-Cohen.cfm goes directly to Bob Cohen's blog within the Bobology website.

Knowing URLs Can Help Your Internet Safety

Knowing a little about how URLs work can help you avoid scams and fraud on the Internet. Sometimes you'll see an email that appears to come from a bank or other organization asking you to update some personal information, with a link to a URL in the text of the message. First of all, no financial organization ever asks for personal or login information in an email. They simply lock you out of your account if something is wrong.

Secondly, these emails, called "phishing" emails, are literally fishing for people who will click on the link in the email and provide the information requested and not bother to check the URL of the web site before entering information. The link in the email doesn't take you to the correct web site. It takes you to a web site that may look like the bank, but isn't the bank's real Web site. To avoid this type of phishing scam, enter the URL you know for your bank or financial institution in your web browser by typing it in.

What is a Search Engine?

A search engine is a type of Web site that specializes in searching the Internet for information. Google, Bing, and Yahoo! are three of the most popular search engines, and they are used every day by millions of people searching the Internet for information.

Using a search engine is pretty easy, and most people using the Internet have done at least one search for something. You've probably done one yourself. In case you haven't, to use a search engine, you go to the main Web site of the search engine, such as www.google.com, then type in a word or phrase. Within seconds, the search engine returns the results of the search on a Web page, and these results are usually a pretty good selection of relevant web sites.

Search engines don't actually go out and scan the Internet for you when you do your search since that would take a lot of time. Instead, search engines are always gathering information about all the Web sites on the Internet. Don't worry, this is all done with software, which never gets tired doing this job. The search engine takes all the information it collects and creates a catalog of its own. When you request a search, it's searching it's own catalog. This is why the search results display in a matter of a few seconds or less.

Many popular search engines of today such as Yahoo and Google started out as simple listings without the ability to search. Instead of catering to each individual, they'd provide a standard list of popular websites on various topics. As computers got more powerful, web developers started cataloging information about as many web sites as possible and creating modern search engines. At the current time, search engines collect information about text and numbers, and media such as photos, videos, and music are cataloged using any text that describes them on a Web site.

Search engines have become very sophisticated at understanding what people are searching for, and will try to deduce what you are looking for based on how you typed in your search. For example, if you type in a search for the word flowers, the search engine is going to think you want to buy flowers, and will display Web sites where you can buy flowers in the search results.   It's actually possible to type in a complete question when you request a search, and the search engine will know that you are looking for an answer to that question. You'll then see results that it thinks are likely to answer your question. Go ahead and give this a try and see if it might help the next time you do one.

Top search engines process billions of searches a day from millions of users around the world on almost every topic imaginable. Many users have their favorite search engine set up, so it is the first thing they see when they go online.

If you ever browse the internet, you've no doubt used a search engine to help you find information, locate specific websites, or just stave off boredom. You can also use search engines to see how popular a website is, and help others find your website.

What is HTML?

The acronym "HTML" stands for HyperText Markup Language, which is the programming language used for creating web pages on the World Wide Web.

HTML is used to tell Web browsers how to display information and content on a Web page. Compared to programming languages used to create software programs, HTML is considered relatively simple. That's because HTML's purpose is to mark up, text and images on a Web page. The formatting instructions, also known as "tags," are hidden so they don't appear on the Web page when it's viewed. So what are these instructions and "tags?"

HTML Formatting and Tags

Let's take a look at something you might know better, like a word processing application on your computer. If you use any type of word processing software, you are probably familiar with formatting options. Things like paragraphs, font sizes, and positioning photos in a document are all ways you can format your document's appearance and layout. Your word processor uses information that you don't see, called formatting tags, to control how your text and images appear. The result is that text and images that are displayed, in the style and layout you chose in the formatting.

Like a word processor, HTML includes it's own set of formatting tags to format text, images, and the layout of these items on a Web page. It's pretty similar in the way your word processor formatting works, it's just designed for Web pages, not sheets of paper.

Browsers Interpret HTML

Browsers such as Internet Explorer, Chrome, Firefox and Safari are software programs that are used to read and interpret HTML in a consistent and standardized way. As you may use the English language to communicate with someone in London, think of HTML as a way to speak to an Internet browser. Using HTML, Web site owners can be sure that their Web pages will be accessible to anyone with an Internet-ready computer. No matter what type of browser someone is using, the universality of HTML code causes the Web page to display the same across different computers, mobile devices, and operating systems.

HTML Standard

HTML is a standardized technology and it's not owned by any one company. It's also free to use. Much like the Associated Press governs the standards for journalistic writing and grammar, the World Wide Web Consortium, or the W3C, maintains the standards for HTML writing and coding. This standardization allows for the consistent interpretation of different elements within the HTML language.

HTML Language

To use the Web, you don't need to know anything about HTML. Your Browser and computer will take care of interpreting the HTML and display Web pages with the correct layout and formatting. But if you plan to use the Web for creating a Web site, blogging, ecommerce, or other activities, learning a little bit of HTML can help you expand your options.

Just as knowing some Swedish might help you on your trip to Sweden, it might also be a good idea to learn some HTML before exploring the nooks and crannies of the World Wide Web. In either case, learning a new language can open up new and unforeseen possibilities and allow you to communicate effectively with people anywhere in the world.

What is a Domain?

"Domain" is a term that is widely used in Internet speak. It refers to a space on the Web that is reserved for a Web site. Just like you have a home, a Web site also needs a home, which is referred to as a domain. To visit a specific

Web page, you must provide a Web address that is unique to it.

How Do Domains Work?

The system of domains on the Web works in kind of the same way as the U.S. postal system works for snail mail. Every house, apartment, store, and location has its own unique postal address, and when you mail a letter to a particular place, its address will take it to that specific unique location.

In the same way, a Web site needs to have a domain name in order to be found. Just as a street address has two parts, the number and the street name, each Web site on the Internet has two parts: the text on the left side of the dot or period; and the text to the right of the dot or period. All domain names must carry both of these parts. The text on the right side of the dot must come from a specific list which is managed exclusively by an international organization called ICANN. Common examples of these used in the United States might include .com, .net, .org, .info, .edu, or .gov. Many additional ones are used internationally, and many countries have their own individual ones that are assigned by ICANN.

Choosing a Domain Name for a Web Site

Choosing an effective domain name calls for creativity, but before you secure that name you must perform a search to ensure that the domain name you want is available ~ that is, it isn't already being used. This search is done through companies that perform domain-name registration. When you request a domain name from one of these companies they will search the internet to ensure that the name is not being used. Yahoo, Go-Daddy, Network Solutions, and many others, as well as companies that host Web sites can do this.

What is a Cookie?

There was a time when a cookie was nothing more than a sweet, round, and flat baked treat you dip in a glass of cold milk. But in the digital age, the word "cookie" has come to mean a whole new thing.

In technology, a cookie is to a small bit of information that is sent from a website you're visiting, then stored in the browser you're using. When you visit that particular website again, it fetches the data saved in the cookie so that the website would know about your past activity. It consists of a set of letters and numbers that identify a specific computer when it accesses the Web. A Web browser, in case you haven't been a subscriber, is the software application on your device that is used to browse and display Web sites. The most common ones are Microsoft's Internet Explorer, Apple's Safari, Mozilla Firefox, and Google Chrome. They are all good, and they all accept and store cookies.

Why Are Cookies Important?

Why is this important? Think about some of the websites you need to log on to, like Facebook, Twitter, or even mine, bobology. It would be inconvenient to have to log in every time you visit -- even if your visits are within the same hour. Wouldn't it be great if these Web sites remember your email address and password? Thanks to cookies, you can make a website store these important bits of data, and get them when needed.

Cookies and Privacy

However, not all cookies are believed to be helpful. Some cookies store what and how you search online, so that third-party advertising companies, social networks, and other Web sites can know exactly what kind of ads will interest you. Many people think this is a major violation to their privacy. But unfortunately it's the price we pay for many of the free services we receive on the Internet. Facebook, Twitter, Google, Bing, and many other Web sites provide services and resources for us for free, but in exchange, when we accepted the terms and conditions for setting up our accounts, we agreed to allow the Web site to track our behavior, and sometimes use our information for targeting ads.

Using Shared Computers and Devices

Other than privacy issues, there's one other side to cookies that can be harmful. If you use a public computer, or share a computer with someone else, a cookie on that computer may think it's you when you visit a shopping cart or commerce site and allow you to login. Other people may end up getting access to your email, social media profiles, etc. if they use the same computer after you're done with it. This is because information pertaining to you is still stored in the cookies. This applies not only to computers, but to smartphones and tablets, since the cookie is stored in the browser application, and all devices use browser software to display Web pages.

Why You Need Cookies

You can't get rid of cookies altogether because many websites don't work properly if you disable them. What you can do is clear your cookies after you finish surfing the Internet. Even if you're sharing your computer with other people, they will not have access to your personal online accounts. Remember, you will probably need to login with your user account and password if any Web site you used stored that information for you, since they probably used a cookie.

Deleting Cookies

Here's a link to an article on cookies which includes links to each browser website with instructions for deleting cookies in each of the popular browsers.
http://www.bobology.com/cookies.html

Here's instructions for Mobile Devices:

Delete Cookies in Apple Safari on iPhones and iPads: tap Settings, then tap Safari, then tap Clear Cookies and Data

Delete Cookies in Chrome for Android: Tap Menu, then tap Settings, then tap Privacy, then tap Clear Browsing Data

What are Bookmarks

Have you ever been reading a book and put in a bookmark to save your place because otherwise you would not remember where you were or what you wanted to come back to? In the technology world a bookmark does the same thing. The internet is an easy place to get lost. You might search for something and end up going through numerous different websites before you find what you are really looking for. If you are on a site that you want to be able to find again easily, you just place your bookmark so that you can come back to it later.

It is very easy to place a bookmark for a web address to which you'll want to return. All you have to do is click on "add bookmark" in the bookmark menu.

Bookmarks on the internet can really make using the internet easier. If you are doing work, writing a paper or just want to remember something later on, you can simply bookmark the page. Then all you have to do to retrieve the page is scroll down your bookmarked list. This is way easier than trying to remember a bunch of different web pages.

What is a Username?

A username is an identity created by the user of an account or online service in order to distinguish himself from other users. It can be the user's real name or a fictitious name that he creates. Other terms for username include sign-on name, screenname (screen name) and user nickname. The term originated in the late 1970s.

If you use any online service or Web site such as online banking or shopping, it's pretty common for you to see a screen that says "Enter Your Username." The username is the text that you enter to start the logon process. While it would be helpful if you could use one username for everything you do on the Internet with all of your accounts, sometimes that's not possible because not all Web sites and online services use usernames the same way. By the way, when I say "account," it refers to any Web, Internet, or mobile service that requires you to use a username.

If you're already using several Web sites and online services, you are probably already using several different usernames on the Internet. So of course, you have to figure out how to keep all of your usernames straight, so you enter the right one for the specific Web site you need to access. There's your email login username, your bank, your Apple ID, and maybe dozens more depending on how involved you've become in using online services. By the way, anyone with a Social Security Number can create an online account at any age and view reports on benefits and earnings. Often, if you don't want to wait on the phone for support, receive updates for the software you use, or avoid waiting in line for a "live" office visit, you're probably going to be using an online account with a username.

So why don't all these Web sites and online services use usernames the same way so you could use just one, and is it really a good idea to have one username anyway? First, let's look at what usernames really are used for by a Web site or Internet service.

Usernames Identify a Unique Individual

A username is unique to the user of an account, meaning that two people using an online account service cannot have the same username. Think of an example of two people who sign up for bank accounts at the same bank; under no circumstances will they ever be given the same account number. Similarly, usernames are always unique. If a user tries to create a username that is already being used, the software that runs the online service will not allow it.

Creating a username will generate a unique identity for you when using the services available from an online account. For example, the email service Gmail requires every user to create a username for her account, which also serves as her email address. Many people use their first and last name plus an initial. Because people's names are not unique (John, Mary, etc.) some people use combinations of their names and random numbers to create a username. Examples of usernames include johndoe, jdoe65, jdlovestofish, alwayssunnyinphilly.

Some online services allow you to create multiple accounts. A good example is Amazon, which is a popular shopping site. Amazon allows you to create multiple accounts, and uses your email address as your username. Use a different email address and you can create a new account. This type of approach allows a person to have one account for personal purchases and another for business purchases. Each account is completely separate from the other account, because it's a different username that's used to login for each account.

Ok, so now we know that a username allows an online service to identify a unique person who uses that service.

Why Can't I Use One Username for Everything?

Some Web sites and online services use an email address for your username and some don't. Technically, either approach works, but services that don't use your email address for your username require you to create a new username with letters and numbers. The becomes your username for the service and is what you use to login whenever you use the service. Sometimes the service limits the number of characters you can use for your username and sometimes they may require a minimum number of characters.

This all gets down to the way the people who created the online service. Some services use your email address and a password to logon, while others require you to create a unique username, and won't allow you to use your email. There are a few reasons why there's a difference.

One reason is that some online services identify you with an existing number or member ID. Things like a Social Security number, health care member ID, student ID, credit card number, auto-club membership, and bank account number are already used to identify someone or someone's account. As a result, sometimes a site will ask you to use that for your username. More often though, the service wants to keep your username more secure, and to do that they require you to create a new username that's different from your account, member, or ID number. Your new username is then used to access your online services.

Some services use your email for your username. The combination of your username and password is required to logon. In this case, your email address and your username are the same thing. Since your email address can be seen by anyone who receives an email from you, it's less secure than a separate username. Often, if a Web site or online service requires people to use something other than an email address for a username, it will discourage some users from signing up to use the service. As a result, Social Networking sites like Facebook, and shopping sites like Amazon let you use your email address for your username. Using an email address makes it easier to signup for the service since there are fewer steps to creating an account with the service.

What Happens to Usernames?

When you use a username to access or logon to a service, your Web browser will sometimes ask you if you want to save the username for that Web site. If your personal computer, phone, or tablet isn't used by anyone else, this is generally considered by security experts to be ok.

If you have saved usernames on your computer, anyone who can access your computer will be able to see and use your username. The best protection for this is to use a password for logging on to your computer. While it's not foolproof, it is a deterrent. Think of it like a lock on your home. A locked door isn't going to stop a determined robber from breaking in if they want to, but it will act as a deterrent, making it more difficult than an unlocked door or window.

Sometimes you may use a public computer or borrow someone else's. If you logon to any account and enter your username, your Web browser displays a pop-up message asking you if you want to save your username. If your borrowing anyone's computer or mobile device, always select NO so your username isn't saved. In this case, your password is your last defense.

It's surprising how many people still use the word "password" as their password, and I've included a link here to the newsletter article on passwords for you to learn more about them.

What is a Strong Password

Lately, some websites requiring passwords have added a new feature to assess your password strength. As you create your password, a field of text may appear on the screen telling you if your password is weak, adequate or strong. The text might change color from red to yellow to green or even prevent you from creating a password that isn't considered strong.

But what exactly is a strong password and why do you need one? First, let's talk about why you need a strong password. According to Digital ID News, the average Internet user has 25 accounts, but only 6.5 passwords. In such a case, if a hacker can get access to one of your passwords, then that hacker can get into several of your accounts. And the weaker your password, the more likely it is a hacker can figure it out.

Many of us also like to use common passwords. Password expert Joseph Bonneau, in a recent interview with National Public Radio, said many people use "password" as a password or numbers in a sequence, like 123456. Nicknames like "princess" or common terms like "qwerty" get used often, too, making it easy for hackers to simply guess at your password.

A strong password is one that is uncommon and hard to guess. It should include a random combination of upper and lower case letters, numbers and special characters. Also, you should not reuse your passwords for numerous accounts.

Many experts recommend a sort of triage for your passwords. Your bank account should have a unique password with multiple characters in a random combination. A password for a site containing very little personal information won't need to be as strong.

Then, too, you also need to protect your passwords. One reason many of us reuse passwords or make them easy to remember is so that we can remember them. Some experts recommend keeping a password wallet or using a password app to keep track of all your passwords. If you use this, then you only need to remember the one password.

Take stock of your passwords. Are they strong? Will they protect you from hackers? If not, it might be time to give your passwords a workout and improve their strength in order to protect you.

What is Streaming?

First of all, let me say that streaming is, basically, broadcasting over the Internet. But as with anything technical, there's always more to it than a simple, one-line definition.

Streaming describes a specific way that video, music, or other media files are delivered to you over the Internet. When "streamed," the video you watch or the music you listen to is sent to you to see or hear while you're connected to the Internet. Without an Internet connection, you cannot view the video or listen to the music. Streaming uses the Internet much like radio or TV uses the airwaves to bring you their content.

So How is Streaming Different from TV or Radio?

To understand the differences, let's look more closely at both of them. When you watch a TV show, the TV is your "player," that is, it plays the television broadcast. The TV also needs a way to receive the broadcast, which would be done through the use of an antenna, cable service, or satellite dish. Radio broadcasts work the same way, using radio waves to transmit the music or audio to your radio.

Both television and radio broadcasts come to you by way of transmission over the airwaves, cable, or satellite signal. On the other hand, streaming. to emphasize what we said at the outset, is broadcasting through the Internet.

What Makes Streaming Possible?

The recent development that has brought us this new capability is the introduction of high-speed Internet connections capable of broadcasting media like video and music. Video, music, and other similar information consume enormous portions of Internet capacity because they are larger types of files than things like email or photos. But fast cable, fiber, and other connections have become readily available to nearly everyone, and now that new cellular speeds are so much faster, it's finally possible to broadcast these types of content easily over the Internet.

What You Get, and Don't Get, with Streaming

Simply watching a show on TV or listening to a song on the radio at the time it's broadcast does not result in a tangible copy of it being available to you to watch or listen to later. You experience it in the moment, then it's gone. Streaming, since it's another form of broadcasting, also doesn't result in a copy of the TV show, movie, or song being available to you.

In contrast, downloading creates a copy of the movie, TV show, music, or audio file on your computer or mobile device. Once you have the content on your device, you can watch or listen to it without the need for an Internet connection, as often as you want, wherever you want. For example, buying a song on iTunes results in a copy of the song being downloaded, by way of the Internet, to your iPhone or iPad; then you can subsequently listen whenever you want without having to connect to the Internet.

How do You Do Streaming?

Streaming is done by going to a streaming Web site on your computer, or by using a mobile streaming app. When streaming on a computer, you'll usually be able to access the content by using the same Web browser you currently use for accessing the Internet, for example, Internet Explorer, Safari, Chrome, or Firefox. Go to the Web site for the streaming service, and you'll have access to the streaming service's content.

Since mobile tablets and smartphones are able to access the Internet, most streaming applications also have mobile apps. Using a mobile app for this service makes it easy to use on common mobile devices like iPhones, iPads, Kindle Fires, Android mobile devices, and Windows 8 phones.

Free or Paid?

There are both free and paid streaming applications available to you. In most cases, the paid version of a streaming application requires a monthly or yearly subscription fee. There are some streaming applications that offer a free version, sometimes with the possibility of an upgrade to a paid version. Others may be free, but offer to sell you a copy of a song or other media in the app, which you can download to keep for your own use.

And some streaming applications only offer a paid version, and no free content is available. Some types of content, like movies, are a higher price type of content, and expensive to transmit because they are large files, so it's rare to find a free streaming service for them. Music is a little more competitive than movies, so it's more common to find free or free trial services for music streaming. TV shows are kind of a middle ground, and whether you can find a TV show available on streaming for free or paid often depends on the popularity of a particular show or series. And last, since the owner of the content controls how it's distributed, certain movies, TV shows, and music may not be available on any streaming service anywhere.

Some Examples of Streaming Services

Music streaming can give you access to a large music library, without the need to purchase individual songs or albums. For example, Pandora, a popular music application for streaming music, plays music from its extensive library of music when you open the app on your computer or smartphone. Remember, you need an Internet connection to play music. Pandora is an example of a streaming application that has both a free and a paid version. The free version is advertising-supported, much like broadcast radio and TV, while the paid version includes more options and is ad-free.

Netflix has both a DVD rental service and a streaming application. Both services require a paid subscription, and there are options for buying them separately or as a mix-and-match service.

Choices Abound

Streaming content is available through many Web sites and apps and can expand the variety and use of your Internet experience. I strongly encourage you to explore and take advantage of the ever-expanding opportunities that streaming offers.

What is Opt-In?

Opt-in means that you have chosen the option of being included in an email newsletter service. When you opt-in, you give the company, person, or organization permission to send you email, usually in the form of a regular newsletter.

The organization that sends emails has a list of people that, for the most part, want to receive the emails. Spam is email that you didn't agree to receive. Remember, if you chose to receive an email newsletter, knowingly or not, it's not considered spam.

The term "opt-in" can have a positive and negative meaning, and it often depends on your point of view. Let's look at what opt-in means for the recipient of an email newsletter first, then we'll look at what it means for the email list sender.

Opt-in for the Email Recipient

For readers of email, there is usually just too much email coming in every day. Some of these emails are probably a list that you are subscribed to receive. Chances are, at some point, you chose to "opt-in" to the email newsletter, whether you know it or not.

These "opt-in" emails choices are sometimes visible, but can also hide in various places on Web sites, emails and order forms. For example, when ordering a product or service from a Web site, you may have glanced over a check-box asking you if you wanted to subscribe to their email list for updates, specials, and announcements.

Web sites have become quite savvy at getting customers to opt-in to their email newsletters. One way you often opt-in without even realizing you have is after you place on online order. At the bottom of the order, a company will often automatically check a box with text similar to "Yes, please send me emails with exciting information about your products."

Another way Web sites get you to opt-in is by requiring you to supply an email address and opt-in before you can access a free service or download a free ebook or software product. And of course, you may also have willingly opted-in to a newsletter before you have seen a copy and then decide you have no interest in receiving it.

Opting-Out

You can opt-out of these emails and take steps to limit automatic opt-ins. First, when placing orders or filling out online forms, be conscious of any boxes with check marks. Companies often automatically select the "Yes" box for you making it your responsibility to uncheck the box.

Many email opt-in subscriptions require that you click on a confirmation link before you actually receive the subscription. Your first email from the list will include a link to a Web page that, when clicked, is your confirmation that you want to receive the email. If you don't confirm, you won't receive the email. If the email newsletter is something you truly want to receive, be sure to look in your inbox and spam folder (if you have one) for this "confirmation" email and click on the link. This "confirmed opt0in" is what I use for my newsletter.

Secondly, seriously consider the tradeoff for supplying your personal email to a company in exchange for a free service. The service isn't actually free. Your personal information is the currency in this exchange.

Lastly, if you have unintentionally opted-in to email newsletters, you can unsubscribe. Open an email from the company and scroll down to the bottom of the page. The email will usually contain a link to unsubscribe from the newsletter.

There is one other kind of email subscription that is harder to unsubscribe from, and that's the kind that requires you login to a Web site and manage your "user preferences." To unsubscribe form these lists you have to login to a Web site where your subscription is managed, then select the option or options to unsubscribe from the email. If you've forgotten your password, look for a link that will recover a lost password, then you can login to manage the subscriptions.

When you see the word "opt," think option. It's your choice, and you can opt to take part or not.

The List Owner's Perspective

When a person opts-in and agrees to receive your email newsletter, you have one of the best ways to stay in touch with them. A subscriber who opts-in has chosen to receive your communications, which means they are already interested in what you have to say (provided you have something of use for them to read). Provide good email content to your readers and your subscriber list will grow, making it a valuable asset, whether you're an author, company, or non-profit.

Most reputable email subscription list owners provide an easy way for subscribers to "opt-out." If you send an email list, please provide a link on your email allowing recipients to easily opt-out because you actually only want subscribers who really want to receive your newsletters. Don't worry about people who unsubscribe, because they wouldn't read the email, and by providing an easy way to opt-out, you avoid complaints about your email being spam.

In case you're interested, the email service I use is aWeber. If you are looking for an email list service and you click on the affiliate link, aWeber will provide me with a small affiliate commission, which will support my training and education efforts.

Social Media

What is a Social Network?

A Social Network is any online community of people or organizations who join the community, connect with other users, and share content and updates with the community.

Most people know Social Networks by their names, which include Facebook, Twitter, and LinkedIn, and are the among the most popular Social Networks. After teaching classes since 2007 on Social Networking (also known as Social Media), I've determined that all of them have three characteristics in common.

The three common features of Social Networks are these: join, connect, and share. Let's take a look at what each of these means and how they create this type of community.

Join

All Social Networks require a person or organization to join them in order to access the features of the community. This means setting up an online account with the Social Network, usually through a Web site. You provide your email address, create a password, and maybe have to supply your name and one or two other pieces of personal information.

After completing this information, which involves filling in a form on the Social Network Web site or mobile application, you receive a confirmation email. This email confirmation is an important step and is used to verify that you can receive their email communications. By clicking on a link in the confirmation email, you verify your account. Now you have joined the Social Network and can use all the features available to users.

It's similar to joining many other membership organizations. In order to receive the benefits available to members, you need to join. A credit union is an example of a membership organization. It provides financial services to it's members, and in order to take advantage of the services available, for example, a checking account, you need to join the credit union and become a member. Credit unions have members, and members have access to member benefits.

Social Networks, since they are online communities, use the Web, email, messaging, and other forms of electronic communications to communicate with members. Once you join, you have access to the member benefits. These benefits typically include the ability to connect with other members of the community and share information with them.

Why Are They Free?

All the major Social Networks are free to join, no money is required. They are, however, profit making organizations, and they make money by selling advertising to organizations that want to reach the members of the Social Network.

The fine print in the terms and conditions you are required to accept when you join a Social Network usually gives the Social Network the ability to collect information about you. This includes your activity while using the Social Network, and also allows them to make money by selling advertising to you. Don't be too shocked though. We are generally willing to give up something for a good deal.

You might have a member card with your grocery store that provides a discounted price on your purchases. In return, the store can collect data on what you buy, when you buy it, and use that to make money by selling shopper information to companies that want to learn more about shopper's behavior. We accept free television shows in return for commercials, and almost everyone has a credit card or ATM card, which include terms which allow the card company to track our use and purchases.

Personal information about you is never shared by Social Networks, but your information is collected so if someone wants to reach men that play golf (like me) the community can give advertisers that option. Your personal information is only used to manage your account by the Social Network and is never shared.

OK, so if you want to join and use the Social Network, you setup your account using your email address, create a name you would use in the community (some require your real name, others don't), and then you can use the features of the community, which includes connecting with other users. So now let's move on to the second characteristic of a Social Network, which is connecting.

Connecting

Since these are, after all, Social Networks, they assume you joined to be social, and not anti-social. The whole point of a Social Network is to find and make connections with other users.

Other users might be family members, friends, work associates, or a business or organization. All of these can have user accounts on Social Network. Ever see or hear ad ad that asks you to "like" something on Facebook or "follow" them on Twitter? That's a brand asking you to connect with them. Some Social Network treat people and brands the same while others have different types of user accounts for a business compared to a person. Let's see how this might work.

People who are users can connect with other people who use the Social Network. You might know someone who is already a user on a Social Network like Facebook, Twitter, or LinkedIn. You probably have their email address already if they are someone you communicate with on a regular basis. The email address of a user is a key part of finding and connecting with other users.

If you know someone's email address, and they are a member of a Social Network you belong to, you can locate them by searching in the Social Network search tool using their email address. You might be able to find them by name, location, school, or work history as well, but the email address is the most efficient way and it avoids making mistakes and connecting with strangers. Every Social Network has a way to search for other people, and others can search for you as well.

Once you find someone you know, you can connect with them. This is where Social Networks are different from each other. A "connection" is different on each Social Network and the how it defines a connection gives the Social Network it's "personality."

Facebook, for example, has people connect to each other as Friends. For two people to become Friends, they both have to agree. So one person sends an invitation, and the other person has to accept it; otherwise they don't become Friends on Facebook. A friend is the same connection whether they are a close friend or a distant one. The term Friend means that Facebook will share information about you that is only visible to other Friends, and that you will be able to see information about your Friends that is only available to view because you are a Friend. I'll go into the information part when I discuss sharing, so please hold on.

Twitter uses the terms "followers" and "following" for connections on Twitter. Anyone can follow anyone else, with no permission required, so Twitter is a lot more public than other Social Networks. The users who follow you are your "followers." Followers receive updates from the users they are following when they view their account.

LinkedIn uses the term "connections" for connections, which allows a user to communicate and view more information about someone that if they were not a connection.

The Social Network you use creates a way for people and organizations to share information that isn't visible without a connection to that user. This way, people and organizations don't have to send every one of their connections information because the Social Network takes care of sending the information to all of the person's or organization's connections.

OK, so this might be hard to understand. Let's say you send out a holiday letter by postal mail to everyone on your holiday card list. Each letter has to be individually addressed, stamped, and delivered. If you have everyone over to your home, you can give them one copy that they can read and view. If you have a sign in front of your house, it's public, but if you have something inside your house that only people you invite in can see, it's more private.

The Social Network you use has rules and resources for what you share with your connections. Facebook requires that you be Friends, Twitter lets anyone follow anyone else, LinkedIn makes your profile mostly visible, but only allows you to send a direct message to another user if you are connected to another user. So now on to what you are sharing.

Sharing

You share two types of information on Social Networks, your profile and your updates. Each Social Network has a unique approach to how much you can include, and how the information for your profile and updates are shared. So let's look at a few common networks and how they share.

Profile Information

What you share is really up to you, but some Social Networks, particularly Facebook, want to collect more information about you, your interests, and your activities compared to other Social Networks. Facebook has a very robust way for you to create a profile about yourself. You can include where you live, where you work, your contact information, and your interests, along with your "Likes." Your Likes are the brands, companies, and organizations that you choose to Like on Facebook.

Twitter gives you 160 characters to describe yourself, so it simply doesn't have room for much information in your profile. LinkedIn is primarily a work related Social Network, so your profile is your work history, experience, and skills. So each site has a little different profile approach. But all of them have "updates."

Updates

An update is a piece of information you publish in your account that is automatically sent to your connections. The information can be some text, a photo, video, or a link to another Web page. You are essentially publishing information on a personal Web site that the Social Network gives you, and they take care of sending a message to your connections letting them know you've got some new information to share. What you share is up to you.

If you want to share information about a vacation, your work, what you eat, who you see, it's totally up to you. People will learn about you by what you share in your updates. So your updates are like a journal you share, but everyone has a personal style and preference for what they share and how often they share. Social Networks usually allow you to share photos, videos, and links to other Web pages in addition to plain text. You don't have to be a writer to share on Social Media. Using a smartphone app from the Social Network, you can share your location with your connections since smartphones have GPS chips.

People and Organizations

Depending on the Social Network, people and organizations may be different types of users, with a different type of connection. When you Like something on Facebook, you are choosing to receive updates from that organization similar to the way you receive updates from your Friends. They don't see any of your personal profile information, or your updates because they aren't your Friend. So Facebook has a way for organizations to create a user account, called Pages, and people can Like a Page. Other Social Networks are similar, but with some subtle differences.

Google+ is pretty similar to Facebook, and organizations can have their own user account, and users can receive updates by following them.

LinkedIn has something called a Corporate Page, that is for corporations and other organizations. People connect with other people, but on LinkedIn, people follow a Corporation. By following a corporation, they can send you a direct message, but you will receive their updates in your LinkedIn account.

On Twitter, all users are the same, whether they are a person or an organization. So organizations have the same space for their profile (160 characters), can have followers, and can follow other users just like a personal user.

Advertising

The Social Networks I've mentioned are businesses that sell advertising. Their goal is to collect as many users as possible by offering free, useful, and interesting services for their members. With many members, advertisers are willing to pay to reach the members. It's similar to a television show like the Super Bowl. If your an organization that wants to reach viewers of the Super Bowl on TV you have to purchase a TV ad from the network that broadcasts the Super Bowl.

Advertisers who want to reach as many users as possible on a Social Network are willing to pay to reach you and other users. This is how Social Networks make a profit and how they are able to offer users like us free services.

The benefits of being able to connect and share information with people who live far apart, in different time zones, or just don't see each other that often make Social Media appealing. Human beings are social, with our families, community organizations, towns, schools, and other activities that bring us together. Social Media is just another way, the electronic way that people can be social.

What is a Viral Video?

Every now and then you will hear that a video went "viral." This term, as with numerous other words in this modern age of technology, has acquired whole new added meanings as it relates to the digital world. In a technological sense, people might presume that viral has something to do with a computer virus. But this is not the case.

When Does a Video Become Viral?

When a video goes viral it has simply become extremely popular. Its exposure on the Internet is growing by leaps and bounds as more and more people discover it and pass it along to other users. An image or an article can also become viral, and the meaning in those cases is the same.

So how many views, or hits, will classify a video, image or article as "viral"? There is no single specific number, but many videos, images or articles deemed to have gone "viral" garner more than a million views in a week or less. The classification is probably assigned more as a result of intensive activity and the rate of growth among users in a relatively short amount of time than of simply how many hits something receives.

How Do Videos Become Viral?

A video that has gone viral will likely be found on a video-hosting website, usually YouTube. Since so many people surf the Internet and enjoy viewing these videos, the news of a funny video travels fast. Some people spread the word by putting links on other websites or in forums, which receive a great deal of traffic. Some people just tell others about it. Those others, of course, will look for it, watch it and pass it along to someone else. Before you know it the page views of this video have skyrocketed, making the video very popular — and very viral.

The Cloud

What is the Cloud?

The Cloud is a term used with more and more frequency to refer to services (both hardware and software) that exist on a network. The most common cloud-based services are accessed via the Internet, but a business can also have its own cloud-based services within a private network as well. The term Cloud itself refers to the cloud-shaped symbol used to depict this service in network topology diagrams.

What Does the Cloud Do?

The most common implementation of the Cloud is through online storage of files. The files are typically accessed through a web browser or by a small program designed to access these files. This means that a user in New York can modify a file that can instantly be accessed by another user in California. That same user can then view the file on any device at any time. Similar to other secure transactions on the Internet such as online banking, the Cloud uses encryption to keep data safe from malicious users.

Benefits of Using the Cloud

Cloud computing is making its way into every facet of both business and personal computing. The benefits to using the Cloud are many. Personal cloud services such as Google Drive and iCloud are allowing users to access data (documents, files, pictures) from anywhere using a smartphone, PC, or tablet. Businesses have begun adapting cloud services as well. Since important files are no longer stored locally on an individual's hard drive, the risk of losing important data due to equipment failure or natural disaster is substantially mitigated. Group collaboration even across international lines is easy to accomplish thanks to the Cloud. Many large software companies have started offering cloud-based services to small and large businesses alike. This drives the cost of doing business down drastically and can provide a more seamless experience.

Although the term may seem ambiguous at first glance, the Cloud is taking technology in a new direction. The benefits of using the Cloud increase daily as companies begin to leverage this technology to keep costs low and work more efficiently. Gone are the days of forgetting an important document at home or at the office. With just a few mouse clicks, that file is available anywhere.

What's a Server and a What's a Client?

Computers that do work for other computers (performing services) are called servers. The computers that ask for the services are called clients. Whether a computer is a client or a server describes the role it plays when performing a computing task. With computers connected together on networks like the Internet, some computers on the network can perform services (servers) for other computers on the network (the clients).
You might not have thought about what happens when you connect to the Internet, but there are computers on the Internet doing work for you. Let's see how clients and servers work in a restaurant.

You're the Client, They're the Server

You've probably eaten a meal at a restaurant where you were seated at a table, and a waiter or waitress took your order, brought you your food, and refreshed your beverage. We sometimes use the term "server" to refer to a waiter or waitress, and they "serve" us our food and beverage.

The server comes out to our table to communicate with us and takes our order. After that, we don't see what they do with the order, but we can assume that it's taken to the kitchen, where food is prepared for our meal. When the food is ready, the server delivers it to us at our table. You're the "client" and the waiter or waitress is the "server." You order food, and it's brought to you ready to eat.

Here's the neat trick though, a server can serve more than one client. You know this because your server has additional customers (clients) at other tables. The resources of the restaurant allow one server to take care of multiple clients. If you understand this, it's easy to understand client-server computing, which works almost exactly the same way.

Computers and Other Types of Clients

A personal computer is a common type of computer client. A PC can work alone, or on a network, like the Internet or your home network. Other types of devices function like computers, only we don't always call them computers. Tablets and smartphones are computing devices that also function as clients. They work alone, or work connected to a network. All of these devices can be clients since being a client means asking a server for something.

A computer client (tablet, smartphone, PC) communicates with other computers using the network. Since computers don't literally "speak' to each other, they exchange data and information using networks. The "server" is a computer located somewhere on the network that prepares information and serves multiple clients, with more resources, just like a restaurant kitchen helps the server take care of multiple tables.

Specialized Servers and Multiple Clients

Now let's go a little further and see how one server can help many clients. Let's start at the restaurant first. If a restaurant is large, it may have a specific person who prepares salads, someone else who serves beverages, and another person for preparing main courses, etc..

We know what's involved in preparing food, so it's easier to understand that there could be more than one food preparer, and that each one may have a specific task. Our waiter or waitress is our server, but they're really working with many other individuals, each of whom are helping to serve our meal. Now let's see how this works when talking about computers.

The Internet and Client-Server Computing

When you use the Internet, you're using client-server computing. The Internet is made up of many computers, connected in a network called the World Wide Web. A computer on the Internet often has a specific function or application, like email, and that is it's only job. If it's job is to do email, it's called an email server. Another computer might be responsible for hosting a Web site, so it's called a Web server. It's just like the restaurant that has a dedicated beverage server, salad preparer, or table server. We don't really care who does the job, as long as our "meal" is delivered correctly.

When you click on a link to a Web page, your computing device is the client computer, and the computer that sends you the Web page is the server computer. As a client, we just want our services delivered to us.The work could be done on one computer or many. We really don't need to know, as long as it's delivered. If a server computer is doing it's job, we get our services (email, Web pages, etc.) delivered to us.

Advantages of Client-Server Computing

One advantage of client-server computing is that it allows a software application to work either on the client, or the server. The people that make the software can use more powerful server computers located in a computer room, and the people using the software only need small devices that can connect to the servers. If the hard work can be done by servers on the Internet, then the client device can be smaller, lighter, and less expensive.

If you've ever used a Web site for a map or directions, you're an experienced client-server computing user. You used your computer to go to the map Web site and then entered two pieces of data, the from address, and the to address. Not much data, just two simple lines of text. The next step is to click on a button that usually says route, or get directions. What you've done is sent two small pieces of data to a Map server on the Internet.

It's the Map server that calculates the directions, prepares the steps and a map, and then sends you a Web page that displays on your computer or mobile device ready to use.Your client doesn't need to store the map database in memory, nor have the computing power to prepare a route. The server did all that for you, usually in a few seconds. Your client waited patiently for the server to do it's work, then it received a Web page and displayed it on your computer or mobile device.

Voila! You're an experienced client-server computing user.

What is Syncing?

The term syncing is short for, and a synonym to, the word synchronizing. Synchronizing in the computer world is the process of matching up two or more copies of information, and updating all of them, so they are identical. When all of your information is identical wherever you use it, it is in"sync."

Synchronization in the Olympics

If you've ever watched the summer Olympics, (I always try to) you might know two events scored on synchronization, synchronized diving and synchronized swimming. I'm not an Olympic event judge, but I know that higher scores are given for those teams that are better synchronized. This makes sense since the goal of the events is to have identical movement and positions for the team members.

For the diving event, it's two people who dive off a platform matching each other's movements, while for synchronized swimming, it's a team. Perfection is achieved when all the movements and positions are the same. Watching a whole team of swimmers go through their routine of synchronized motions and positions while is a challenge since so many team members are involved, and all of them need to be identical. Now let's move to the world of computers.

Synchronization for Computers

Your computer is an electronic device with some form or storage of information on it, like a hard drive or flash memory. It doesn't matter what the data or information is for our discussion, so it could be a set of contacts, or a list of products, or a document. If there is a copy of that information located on another computer, when one copy is updated or changed, the copies become out of sync, unless there is a way to update the information so it becomes identical again. The swimmers have a coach to help them stay in sync, and your data needs a coach too. The coach is a software program that performs the synchronization. Let's see how this is done.

Software Does the Work

Synchronizing two or more copies of information with each other requires software that can see the changes are on each copy, compare them, then update all the copies contain the same information.

For example, if your computer has a list of contacts with phone numbers, first and last names, and addresses, you might want to use that list of contacts on your smartphone or tablet, or even between a desktop and a laptop, or possible on all of these devices.

One way to synchronize the information is to use a cable to connect each device to the computer, then use software which will "sync" the data and match the two copies. This requires that each device be connected to your computer to do the sync. Here are some common ways you might even have done to sync data.

iTunes is a commonly used desktop software program that has been used with iPod music players for years to synchronize information between computers and iPods. Some of my readers may remember devices called Palm Pilots and using a cable and software provided by Palm to do the sync.

Adding More Devices for Sync

Just like with synchronized swimming, as you add more devices that you want to keep in sync with each other, the effort to do so can make it more difficult. One way is to connect your smartphone, tablet, MP3 player, and laptop to your main computer and sync each one by using a cable connection. Another way is to copy a file from one computer or device and move it to another using a flash drive. (I still have some floppy drives and Zip drives too).

But with modern mobile devices, data can be moved wirelessly using networks like WiFi and cellular. In order to move and synchronize data wirelessly, you still need to make a wireless connection between each device, so this would be the same as doing it by cable, except wirelessly. But, there is another way.

What a Master Copy Does

If you keep a master copy of your data or information on a computer that is always available on the Internet, then it's possible to use that computer to be your "master" copy of data for all of your devices. When your laptop, desktop, smartphone, or tablet connect to the Internet, each one checks in with the master copy of the information. Your device sends any updates and changes you made on it to the master copy, and the master copy sends any updates and changes it has to your device.

Using a master copy of data and information, and updating and changing it from each device, is one function of the cloud. When using a cloud service, you keep a master of your contacts, email, calendar appointments, photos, documents, files, and other information in one location.

It's just that the master copy isn't on your desktop any longer, it's on a computer located on the Internet, or what is called the cloud. Your desktop becomes another copy of the data and information, but the cloud takes care of updating your desktop just as though it were any other device you use for a copy of that information.

More Tech Terms for Free

Each week I explain a new technology term in my bobology newsletter. To subscribe go to the bobology website at **www.bobology.com** and use the email newsletter form in the upper right.

The email newsletter is completely free and you can always unsubscribe at any time by clicking on an unsubscribe link. This way you'll be able to keep up with the ever changing language of technology.

www.ingramcontent.com/pod-product-compliance
Lightning Source LLC
LaVergne TN
LVHW052302060326
832902LV00021B/3668